Gabe provides something we all could use more of! And that's clarity around our purpose and meaning. In a place of dehydration, his words read like a fresh drink of water. I'm buying multiple copies to give to friends immediately!

JEFFERSON BETHKE, *New York Times* bestselling author of *Jesus > Religion*

Each page is raw, unfiltered, and real. A truly special book that will challenge your approach to life.

JEREMY SHADA, actor, artist, and songwriter

There is power in authenticity and vulnerability, and Gabe gifts that to his readers in spades. In sharing his struggles, from walking the valleys of depression to embarking on the journey to embrace failure as opportunity, he doesn't hold back. While Gabe's story is truly one of a kind, the themes are universal and relevant to today's generation in a big way.

MATT JAMES, star of *The Bachelor* season 25

A Mission for Meaning is a true testament to faith and grace for oneself. Gabriel's ability to paint the picture of an imperfect man doing his best to show up for his loved ones and himself is inspiring and relatable. From the beginning to the end of his story, you get a view into ups and downs, highs and lows, leaving you rejuvenated in your own faith.

SYDEL CURRY-LEE, creator and mental health advocate

A Mission
for Meaning

A Mission
for Meaning

The Choices That Lead to the Life You Really Want

GABRIEL CONTE

WITH MARK DAGOSTINO

ZONDERVAN
BOOKS

ZONDERVAN BOOKS

A Mission for Meaning
Copyright © 2022 by Conteam, LLC

Requests for information should be addressed to:
Zondervan, *3900 Sparks Dr. SE, Grand Rapids, Michigan 49546*

Zondervan titles may be purchased in bulk for educational, business, fundraising, or sales promotional use. For information, please email SpecialMarkets@Zondervan.com.

ISBN 978-0-310-36424-5 (audio)

Library of Congress Cataloging-in-Publication Data

Names: Conte, Gabriel, 1994- author. | Dagostino, Mark, author.
Title: A mission for meaning : the choices that lead to the life you really want / Gabriel Conte, Mark Dagostino.
Description: Grand Rapids : Zondervan, 2022.
Identifiers: LCCN 2022022461 (print) | LCCN 2022022462 (ebook) | ISBN 9780310364221 (hardcover) | ISBN 9780310364238 (ebook)
Subjects: LCSH: Motivation—Religious aspects—Christianity. | Intentionality (Psychology) | Self-actualization (Psychology)—Religious aspects—Christianity. | Conte, Gabriel, 1994- | Hispanic Americans—Biography. | BISAC: SELF-HELP / Motivational & Inspirational | SELF-HELP / Personal Growth / Success
Classification: LCC BV4599.5.M66 C66 2022 (print) | LCC BV4599.5.M66 (ebook) | DDC 155.2—dc23/eng/20220720
LC record available at https://lccn.loc.gov/2022022461
LC ebook record available at https://lccn.loc.gov/2022022462

Cover photo: Andrew Joseph Woomer
Interior photos: Shutterstock and 123RF
Interior design: Sara Colley

Printed in the United States of America

22 23 24 25 26 27 28 29 30   /LSC/   12 11 10 9 8 7 6 5 4 3 2 1

To my beautiful wife, Jess, and my newborn baby girl.

Jess, I wouldn't be half the man I am today if you weren't in my life. Thank you for encouraging me, pushing me, partnering with me, and being the most obvious picture of what Christlike love and kindness mean through your clear physical representation of it day in and day out.

My baby girl, Makaiah, thank you for already changing my heart and mind in so many ways I didn't think were possible—the way I think about life as a husband to your mother, as a father to you, and as a man trying to be a light in this seemingly dark world. Though I finished writing this book right before you were born, your presence in my life for those nine months changed me, and changed what I had to share, in ways I cannot explain. Thank you. I love you both with everything inside me.

Contents

INTRODUCTION

A Note from Me to You

Jess and I recently built a house together near the beach, not far from where I grew up. We're both fortunate to have thriving careers. We're expressing ourselves and our passions online through videos and music and other creative outlets. I'm living out other entrepreneurial dreams too, investing in real estate and launching other businesses. I'm close to my parents. I have a circle of longtime friends who support me through good times and bad. I have my health, which is a miracle in and of itself given my family history. I'm married to one of the most amazing women on the planet. And I'm grateful that many of these blessings came into my life before I was twenty-five years old.

In many ways, I have more success in my life than any man could ever ask for.

I would hate for any of this to come across as boasting. That's not what I'm trying to do. I'm trying to share this success in the best way I know how: by telling my story in hopes that it inspires positive change, or at least brings some encouragement, in your life too. I want the rest of my generation to know that a good life, a *great* life, an exceptional and purposeful life, the life you thought you could only dream about, is possible. Even if you're struggling (I'm in my own mental valley as I write this). Even if there's trouble in your family history that you feel might be holding you back. Even if you're battling depression, as I have in the last few years. Success—however you define it—can be yours. At any age. And you can begin to earn it and achieve it and *live it* right now by making decisions about what you want—what you *really* desire—from this miracle of life you've been given.

I know that sounds optimistic, and it may be hard to believe. At times, I even have to remind myself that it's true. Most days I don't feel any different from any other twentysomething. Especially in the middle of the struggles we're all going through right now. It seems like all we ever hear is *bad news*. Every minute of every day we're reminded about how much debt we're in and how depression and anxiety rates are skyrocketing. We hear about poverty rates around the world and down the street. We always seem to be on the brink of another conflict, if not another war. And don't even get me started on the current political climate. Just turning on the news or scrolling through social media is enough to make most young people believe life is over before it's begun.

I'd argue it's not true. It's all about perspective.

My point in writing this book is to share a little *good news* for once. To tell you that life is pretty amazing when you commit to making it so. The world hasn't turned its back on us. America still offers every opportunity that young entrepreneurs (including minorities and immigrants from all around the world, my family included) have dreamed about and turned into reality for generations. I can say this because I'm doing it.

And getting here wasn't an accident.

Everything you want in life doesn't just get handed to you. To find fulfillment and success, I know firsthand that you have to be accountable for the consequences of your own actions—how you treat your dreams, your relationships, and your own heart too. And treating those things well requires paying attention to your beliefs and choices every step of the way.

That's not easy. Shaping the kind of family you want, the career you want, or the impact you want to make on the world takes work. It takes dedication. It takes sacrifice—although, I've got to tell you, it doesn't feel like much of a sacrifice when you realize that giving up some immediate gratification here and there leads to landing where you want to end up.

If there's one thing I've learned, it's that arriving at the kind of life you want takes setting goals and making bold choices.

It takes intentionality.

By the way, *intentionality* is one of Jess's favorite words, and I mention it a lot in this book, so I have to give my wife credit. I totally stole it from her.

JESS: Steal it. Use it. Seriously. More people need to hear it.

GABRIEL: Okay. I will.

JESS: Thanks!

Don't worry. You'll hear more from Jess later.

Which brings me to another thing I've learned: carefully choosing who you surround yourself with *matters*. You can't do life alone. We all need partners and friends, mentors and teachers. These people will teach you and influence you in many ways—for better or worse, whether you're aware of it or not—which is why it's important to look for people you admire and want to emulate. Having the *right* people on your side helps you keep your eyes on the prize, so to speak, which means it's important to choose carefully. If you watch me on YouTube, you've probably heard me say, "Show me your friends and I'll show you your future." I say it because it's true.

Now, I won't pretend I have all the answers you're looking for, because I don't. Like you, I'm still figuring it out. That is part of the journey we're all on: to lead a life full of meaning and joy and purpose. To me, that journey—the journey to find meaning, joy, and purpose—is the mission that matters most.

Finding purpose needs to be purposeful. It requires making choices.

I've chosen, very intentionally, to live my life a certain way. And because of the choices I've made, I'm living a purposeful life. I've already achieved many of the things high school me could only dream about. Which is still kind of weird, honestly. I often have to pinch myself. I don't want to sound like I'm bragging. But I cannot pretend that where I am in life is merely due to luck.

Before I continue, if you think I have the "perfect" life, please know it certainly hasn't been all perfect. It's been a struggle, starting way back before I was born. And I've had my share of ups and downs like anyone else. But a few differences in the way my parents chose to live, the way they chose to raise me, and the way I've chosen to live made a huge difference in their lives and mine.

Simple changes made a big difference, and they can make a big difference for you too.

There *is* a playbook I've used—a playbook for life that's been around for a very long time—which I've done my best to understand and learn from. (Hint: It's called the Bible.) I mention this because the Bible has influenced me and many of the decisions I've made, so I'm not going to ignore its impact on my life. But much of what I've learned and applied is practical and can make significant positive changes in your own life, whether you believe in Jesus or not. So while my goal in this book isn't to lecture you or tell you what to do, I do want to share stories of how faith-centered choices have shaped my life and brought me to where I am.

The best way I know to explain why I've been successful, really the *only* way I know how to share my so-called secrets of success, is to share stories from my journey so far: highs, lows, ups, downs, missteps, big decisions, small choices, breakthroughs, and miracles.

Like I said, success doesn't happen by chance. You can't coast forever on one choice, one decision, one lucky break, or one great moment. True success, which is about a lot more than making money, comes from the dozens of little choices you make every day. It's pretty simple, really: the more you choose things that are good for you—not just in the moment but also in the big picture of who you want to be and what you want to accomplish in life—the more fulfilling your life will be. This applies to dating, relationships, marriage, friendships, work, school—everything.

Living intentionally early in life is sort of like investing in a retirement account—it's investing in your future. And the earlier you start, the more value and compound interest you'll accumulate along the way. And it's never too late to get started. Ever.

The problem is we're all faced with a million distractions and temptations every day that take us off course. Through the media, our peers, even the music we listen to and social media, we get the impression that everything sucks and there's no hope for our generation. Whether we realize it or not, we continually deal with information overload, mental overstimulation, and comparison. All this negative noise constantly bounces around in our heads, and it's so loud! It's super hard not to fall prey to it. It's easy to fall into bad habits when negativity and dishonesty bombard us. But what a lot of us seem to forget (me included sometimes) is it's entirely up to us to choose what our relationship with the world looks like. It's up to us to turn away from the noise, to turn our phones and TVs off when we need to, to schedule time for what's important so we can focus on what's real, what's possible, and what's *good for us.*

I am positive I would not be successful in any way that matters to me if I hadn't been intentional about the choices I made. I wouldn't have the influence I have. I wouldn't have the friends and community I have. You wouldn't be reading this book! And I know for sure that Jess wouldn't have married me if I weren't the man I chose to be in the decisions I made along the way—long before we met.

Does that mean I'm perfect? Absolutely not. I've battled depression. I've faced temptation—and lost to it often. I've made bad decisions, I've messed up. But what's important is that I learned from those moments. I analyzed. I spent time reflecting and heeding perspectives from others I trusted. And I adjusted.

Am I a "lucky" guy? Sure, if that's how you want to see it. I just don't think "luck" is totally random. It's more like the possible result of making every effort you can. I mean, you can't get lucky if you don't try, right? This means you have to actually try to get what you want if you want a shot at getting it. Things won't always work out. Nothing is guaranteed.

But I'm here to show you it's *possible*.

It doesn't matter how many times you've fallen, or how far off-course you've gone, or how miserable you might have felt as recently as just a few minutes ago—right before you picked up this book. I'm here to tell you that you can get back up, get back on track, step onto a new path (if that's what you want), and have confidence about where you're headed.

I can't wait to share with you, through the example of my life so far, that you (yes, *you*) have the ability to choose to live differently, to love differently, to do *everything* more successfully, more positively, more abundantly, and more intentionally—starting right now.

ONE

Failure Equals Opportunity

Jess and I had recently moved into a new condo in Los Angeles, the first place we ever bought together. It was right around the time of our first anniversary, and we were just hanging out, enjoying our new home, talking about something random when the conversation became a bit more serious. Out of the blue, Jess started bawling her eyes out.

"What's wrong? What's the matter?" I asked.

"I'm so homesick," she said.

"I know. I wish there was more I could do."

"This just isn't fair," she said, sounding helpless.

She was so upset.

Neither of us knew that when Jess left the house where she grew up in Australia to move in with me in LA, she would be stuck in America. To make a long story short, our first immigration lawyer submitted the paperwork incorrectly, which meant Jess's application ended up under review for a year and a half longer than the process should've taken. At the time, we didn't know what the holdup was, but it probably wouldn't have been so bad if he hadn't *also* forgotten to submit the additional document that would've granted her the ability to travel while her application was under review. She wasn't allowed to leave the country and go back to see her family. We'd been dragged into a nightmare of red tape for almost a year when this conversation happened, and through tears, she told me, "I just can't take it anymore!"

Until that moment I had no idea the extent to which Jess was so upset about all this—and so upset with *me*.

JESS: I don't know why I didn't let it all out before then, but holding it in was definitely not the right thing to do. I let my emotions build up way too much, and then everything came pouring out all at once. It shocked him. And that's never a good way to start a conversation. It's a really good way to start a fight.

I immediately got defensive and pushed back: "What are you talking about?" I asked. "You said you always wanted to live in America! I don't understand."

"I want to go home," she said. "I just want to *leave*."

Her words just about crushed me. I took them personally. I heard them in the worst possible way. I felt like she was rejecting me. I wondered, "Why did you even come here if you hate it so much? If the US sucks this bad, then why did you decide to *live* here? We've barely been married a year and now you're telling me you want to *leave me*?"

When Jess came at me with this flood of feelings and capped it by saying she wanted to "leave," all I could see was a blinding white light of sadness and confusion and fear. I didn't want to listen to her. I didn't want to hear what she was saying. So instead, I responded as if I were being attacked, and in the heat of the moment, I said some things I truly didn't mean.

These are the parts of life the public never sees: what happens behind the social media facade that always makes things look perfect and happy.

Our wedding celebration in Australia was a dream. We were surrounded by family and friends, and after a day full of rain, the sun burst through the clouds and gave us the most beautiful sunset. (Just kidding. It rained the whole day, lol! But it really was everything either of us could've asked for.) The year after that went by quickly, filled with all the moments you get to share together as newlyweds.

But what happens once the honeymoon phase is behind you? When time passes and real life sets in? Growing up, we're all given the false impression that every good relationship leads to everlasting joy, as if meeting "the one" makes everything perfect and easy and peaceful. I guess I held on to that false impression myself because this sudden turn in our marriage took me entirely by surprise.

I thought things had been going really well for us.

JESS: They *had* been going really well for us. That wasn't what I was upset about.

I ran through a checklist in my mind. We loved being married. We loved living together and working together and finally getting to be around each other all the time without any distance between us. (Dating long-distance on two separate continents wasn't easy!) Our careers were growing. We were making good money. We had friends in the city. We were so blessed! I thought we were happy.

Honestly, I wasn't entirely clueless that Jess was struggling. As the months went on, I had a hunch that something might be wrong with Jess and that she might not be happy with her relationship with this country. But I thought if I ignored it, the problem would resolve itself—never a good idea, by the way—and that time would help Jess slowly make this country her home. Clearly that was not the answer.

So the argument intensified. I said things. She said things. I raised my voice and she raised hers until we finally couldn't stand it anymore. Well, I couldn't. I was so upset I grabbed the keys and was about to walk out the front door. Jess begged me to stay. She was so hurt seeing us like this and wanted to resolve it then and there. I, on the other hand, was too upset. I walked out the door anyway. I went for a drive to have some space to myself for a bit. Once I pulled out of the garage, I knew I should give this situation to God, pray about it, and allow God to give me some clarity. If you're a Christian who believes in the power of prayer, you know the drill. And you might even know what it feels like to do what I did next: the exact opposite. I kept driving, stayed stubborn, and tried to come up with arguments that would show Jess how right I was and ways I could fix the problem myself! (Because I was clearly doing a fantastic job so far.)

It took a while (and I mean *a while*) to finally calm down and really *think* and to pray about the situation and understand what Jess was really saying.

As I calmed down, I realized she wasn't telling me that she wanted to leave *me*. She never said that. She just wanted to *leave*. She wanted to see her family. She wanted this agonizing residency fiasco to be over.

I wanted those things too. I should've had my eyes open enough to realize that *the situation* was what I was fighting. Not Jess. But my defensive knee-jerk reaction made Jess even more upset than she was in the first place. And seeing her more upset made *me* more upset. Only I wasn't upset *for* her, as I should have been, I was upset *at* her for making me feel guilty and responsible for her pain. I took what she said personally, like it was my fault for putting Jess in this situation.

Or maybe, more than anything, I was upset with myself. Sometimes you don't realize how selfish you can be until you're forced to look in the mirror.

Either way, it was awful.

We'd had some little disagreements since we first moved in together, like any new roommates or couples might as they adjust to each other's habits and routines, but this was something else. This wasn't a misunderstanding. It wasn't a mistake. It's not like I left the toilet seat up or something. This wasn't the sort of thing that could be fixed with some flowers and an "I'm sorry. I'll do better next time." The girl I loved more than anyone else in the whole world was hurting, and I had minimized and disregarded her feelings. I made myself the victim.

That was on me.

Dealing with struggles, with differences, with anger, with emotional conflict is hard. If you're not on the same page as your partner, if you're not following the same playbook, if you're not truly committed to the vow to stay together—till death do us part—you can easily spend so much time fighting each other that you lose the battle. But your partner is not who you should be fighting in the first place.

Letting this one fight spiral into resenting each other wasn't what either of us wanted. I knew that. She knew that. And I knew we both needed to learn a better way to deal with these feelings. I mean, we didn't have a choice, right? We *had* to get better if we didn't want to lose each other. And we were both committed to never losing each other.

Dealing with conflict in a relationship is kind of like going through an intense workout at the gym: If you do the workout right, it will make you stronger. If you don't, you'll get hurt.

Jess and I are obviously still together. We didn't break up. We were able to get through that fight after our first year together, and she is at my side as I work on this book. But the struggle over how to deal with our families living on opposite sides of the planet is a conversation that comes up again and again. It became a huge issue once more during the pandemic, and we're still trying to figure it out to this day.

So how did we manage this part of our marriage without breaking up?

Getting past that first big fight didn't just magically happen, and resolving the conflict and getting on the same page again wasn't a result of one simple piece of advice someone told us or a tip we learned. There are no shortcuts to resolution. The way we got through it was based on a mutual decision: *the decision to look at our failure as an opportunity*.

I'm going to come back to this story. Later in this book I'll share the details of how we got through it—because I really want you to understand them.

Knowing how to deal with this stuff prevents potential areas of conflict from dictating your entire relationship and makes life more enjoyable. It allows you to get back to the good stuff. The moments you'll fondly remember. The love, the excitement, the happiness, the partnership. The kind of success you want in your relationships and, really, in your whole life.

To explain how we find and create those opportunities, and how you can do it too, it's important that you understand more about who we are as people and how we got to where we are. And because I'm sure Jess will write a book about her own life story someday, I will use these pages mostly to help you better understand *me*, which I hope will inspire you to want to better understand *yourself*.

For that, I need to go back to the beginning. Or before the beginning. I need to go back to a time *before* I was born to tell you the story of my parents. Because if it weren't for the choices *they* made, I wouldn't even be here. I wasn't *supposed* to be here.

I'm not exaggerating when I tell you that it's a miracle I'm alive and well.

And that miracle set the stage for *everything*.

TWO

Miracles

I was ten years old when my parents called me into their bedroom, telling me they wanted to talk. I remember it was dark out, and they both seemed serious. I was worried that maybe I'd done something wrong.

They sat me down on the edge of the bed, and they were silent for what felt like the longest few seconds of my life. They looked at each other, then looked at me. Finally my mother said, "Gabby"—that's what my parents and siblings and early childhood friends all call me, even today—"we have something we want to tell you. And we don't want you to be scared—"

"There's no reason to be scared," my dad jumped in. "You're old enough now to hear this and understand it, that's all."

It's the norm in my family for everybody to jump in and talk over each other, and it was no different that night.

"Right. This isn't anything new," my mom said. "We've known about this since before you were born."

"And you're safe," Dad said. "You're okay, and your *mom's* okay, it's just—"

"Before you were born, before your brother was born, I was diagnosed with a disease. And thank God it wasn't passed on to you or Claudio. But—"

"What your mother is trying to say is—"

"I'm HIV positive."

As a ten-year-old, I had never heard about HIV.

They started explaining what HIV was and what it meant, and

I think I zoned out of the conversation until it sunk in that my *mom* had this thing they were talking about.

I looked at her and felt tears welling up in my eyes. I finally opened my mouth to ask a question, but I couldn't get the words out. "Does this . . . does this mean you're . . ."

"No! Honey, no," my mom said, wrapping her arms around me. "I'm fine. I've been fine. I'm on medication. God has been so good to me. To all of us. I don't even feel sick. It's just—"

"There are just a few things you need to know now that you're old enough," my dad said. "Like we have to be careful so that you and your brothers and sister don't contract the virus. It's passed through the blood, so you can't ever borrow your mother's toothbrush because there's a chance her gums could bleed. Even if it's only a little, that could get passed on to you through *your* gums."

Gross!

"I'm never gonna use mom's toothbrush," I said.

"Right! Good," my mom said. "It's just stuff like that."

"We just have to be more careful than a lot of other people about certain things," Dad said. "If your mom ever gets a cut, you need to let us handle it and not try to help in a way that could put you in danger by putting you in contact with her blood. That's all. We've been watching out for you all these years, and we just want you to be aware so you can be careful about it yourself."

"Oh," I said. I thought about it for a few seconds. "But you're gonna be okay?"

"I'm okay," she said.

You never know what you don't know, until somebody tells you.

Learning that I'm the child of an HIV-positive parent was not exactly minor news. I suppose if I hadn't been raised with faith, I might have been overwhelmed by fear and worry. But by that age, I was confident in my relationship with God, at least as much as a ten-year-old could be, and I believed that everything would work out according to God's plans. (I'll talk more about my faith and how I came to it in upcoming chapters.) Or maybe I was just a little naive about how serious the diagnosis was. I don't really remember. But I do remember that I didn't fully freak out.

In the moment, I didn't think to ask my mom how she got it, or about the fact that she knew she had it before I was born, or what it meant for my dad, or *anything* really. I was tired. I just wanted to get ready for bed.

It wasn't until years later that I started to put the whole story together, realizing what a miracle it was that my mom didn't get sicker and that *I* didn't get sick, or worse.

When my mom got pregnant with my older brother Claudio, a lot of people believed a woman who was HIV positive shouldn't have kids. Doctors and friends told her that the best way to avoid any risk of passing HIV on to her baby was not to have a baby at all.

I can't even imagine how Jess and I would feel hearing those words.

My parents ignored everyone's advice to abort her first pregnancy, and when my brother Claudio was born and appeared to be fine, they all told her she was lucky. "You definitely shouldn't risk another one," they said.

Just a few months later they were pregnant again. And against more personal and professional advice, they also decided to keep their second-born child: *me*.

If my parents hadn't followed what God told them, if they hadn't been intentional about their convictions and their faith, *I wouldn't be here*.

The older I get, the more I realize it goes deeper than that: If my parents hadn't gone through the experiences they went through, if they hadn't made the decisions they made to change their lives and raise me the way they did, I would not be the person I am today. If you've seen Jess and me on YouTube or anywhere else, you can't help but see that we're pretty straight edge. We're not huge partiers. Neither one of us ever slept around. (More on that later!) You may think we're boring, but we love our life.

My parents? Yeah. They weren't like that. In fact, the more I learn, the more I realize they were both kind of wild when they were younger—so much so that my dad used to describe himself and his friends as a pack of wild dogs! It wasn't until they were in their mid to late twenties when they both, for very different reasons, made some decisions that changed their lives, and mine, forever.

• • •

My mom, Grace, was born in New Orleans, but her mom is from Colombia, and her dad is from Spain. They met in Venezuela and moved to New Orleans before finally settling in Miami in 1972, and that's where my mom was raised from the time she was eight years old.

> **GRACE:** Gabriel's grandfather, his father's father, always used to say, "If you hang out with sh––, you're going to get smeared."
>
> I wish I had met him sooner. I might have paid more attention.
>
> When I was in high school, my first boyfriend started dealing drugs. He was not a good influence on me, in a lot of ways, and that first relationship is always so impactful. Most people in high school dated, broke up, and moved on to somebody else, but I wasn't like that. I was loyal, and our relationship was

intense. I became needy and felt like I always needed someone by my side, so we were together till I went away to college. I knew I would wind up in jail with him if I kept hangin' out with him. I had to physically distance myself from him because I couldn't seem to break up with him otherwise. So I went to the farthest college I could that was still in state, which was all I could afford. I went to Florida State University (FSU) in Tallahassee, which is about a seven-hour drive from Miami.

Once I was at college, I went to the opposite end of dating. I met a guy who was premed and then got accepted into medical school. He was very smart and we had a lot of fun together, so I married him. I married him when I was still in college and then followed him to med school, in Fort Lauderdale, without finishing my own degree. That marriage lasted only a year before he told me he didn't want to be with me anymore, so we separated, and it took another year until we were finally divorced. By that time, it was 1988.

I was devastated and depressed. I lost it. I got wild. I went from one relationship to another to another to another. It's hard to even talk about that time in my life because now I'm joyful and filled with the Holy Spirit and I love my husband. So when I tell you about my past, I feel like I'm talking about another person. By 1991 I ended up dating a tall, good-looking guy (who shall remain nameless). One day we were watching TV, and we heard that Magic Johnson had been diagnosed with AIDS. It was big news at the time. Here he was, a well-known, heterosexual person diagnosed with this disease that most people assumed was affecting only gay men, and mostly white gay men. AIDS had already killed many people in the gay community, including in Miami, where I was living and working . . . and partying.

The next day, I had a doctor's appointment. I'd had some blood taken in order to qualify for health insurance, and they had called to say I failed one of the tests. I had no idea why. I was healthy. I exercised all the time. Exercise is what saved me from my depression and got me through everything. So I had no idea what they were going to tell me. When I got to my appointment, they said I had tested positive for HIV.

They told me that based on everything they knew, I had maybe ten years to live.

I was a mess. I couldn't believe it. I came home and told my boyfriend, and he seemed as shocked as I was. "Wow," he said. Then a week or so later, he started getting really sick. I was naive. I was so stupid. I'd go visit him at the hospital and ask the nurses, "What does he have? Can somebody tell me? What's his diagnosis?" But no one would tell me.

Since I knew I had HIV, I forced him to get tested, and he tested positive—and then he blamed it on me. "I got it from you!" he said. But it didn't take long to find out the truth: this guy had flat-out lied. He knew he had HIV, and he kept it from me the whole time we were together. I had judged a book by its good-looking cover: He was handsome and tall and well-dressed. His appearance was impeccable—so much so that I had no idea that he was an IV drug user. I'd been blind to it until it was too late.

I got "smeared" in the worst way imaginable.

At that point, I left. I had really messed up, and I felt empty inside, like my heart was full of holes I didn't know how to fill. I had nowhere to turn, and I realized I needed to go back to my mom and my dad. I was twenty-six, and I didn't tell my parents why I needed to move back home. They just took me in. But my mother knew something was wrong, as mothers do, and she went through my files and found my positive test result.

"Grace, is this true?" she asked me. I nodded and she burst into tears. She was devastated.

What I didn't realize is that while I was away, my mother had found God.

I was raised Catholic. I went to Catholic school when I was a little girl in Venezuela and then briefly when we lived in Spain for a year, but I'd been in public school since we'd lived in Miami, and we never went to church. I was baptized as an infant and I went through First Communion, but I was never confirmed, and I never really knew God. I had a sort of Catholic guilt, a fear of God, or a healthy respect for God, and I prayed to God when I was in trouble. But I didn't understand what it meant to have a relationship with God. So I was surprised when my mom went to two of her close Catholic friends who were living for the Lord. These were prayerful women. And they gave her a few prayers that were printed on cards. And these prayers, she passed on to me. I still have no idea how this happened, or why it happened the way it did, but I ended up with a prayer that filled every hole in my heart. Every hole in my being was filled. I was filled with joy. Here I was, given ten years to live, and my parents couldn't understand the joy. I said, "It's God. It's God that's in me."

A verse in the Bible says, "Better is one day in your courts than a thousand elsewhere" (Psalm 84:10). And that was it. I didn't care if I had ten years or five years or if I died tomorrow with this joy I had been searching for my whole life—through relationships, through drinking, through drugs, or whatever. I had finally found it. I would close my eyes and sense that God was with me, and I was finally home. It was a joy unspeakable.

I had spent all that time searching for joy, thinking I would find it in South Beach (in Miami). I always had to have the cutest dress and to go to this club opening and that club opening. But I was never happy. And now? Through prayer, I found that I was content at home, curled up, reading a good book on a Friday or Saturday night.

That all happened in a matter of months—less than a year between my diagnosis and finding God and my whole life turning around. It's amazing how fast everything can change. I decided to turn my passion for exercise into a career. I became a certified fitness instructor and found work at a private gym.

And that's when I met him . . .

My dad, Jean Claude (who goes by J.C.), had moved to Miami from New Jersey when he was just a kid. His parents had immigrated to America to escape from the rise of Communism in Cuba during the revolution of 1958. My dad was born a few years later, and by the 1990s, he held a degree in exercise physiology from the University of Florida. (Go Gators!) He put his degree to work at that private gym, and he was taken with my mom from the moment she walked in through the doors . . .

J.C.: She liked to exercise. I liked to exercise. So I asked her to work out with me and to go jogging with me. We went on these jogging dates, down to the pier and on the beach. And then we went on these twenty-mile bike rides together. I really liked her, and even though I had a girlfriend when we first met, I knew I was all in. I didn't think anything could stop me from pursuing her.

I had been married before too. For two years. In college. And that relationship was a nightmare. We fought all the time, sometimes till five in the morning, even when I had to be to work at 6:00 a.m. When she got pregnant, my rationale was, "Why would I bring a child into this nightmare? It's bad enough with two people. Why have three?" So I convinced her to get an abortion.

We divorced after that, but the divorce—as painful as it was—wasn't what weighed on my heart. The amount of guilt I carried from the abortion was unbearable, and it had been my idea. I wanted it to happen. I privately nicknamed myself "Dr. Death." I'm convinced it was a boy. I don't know why, but in my spirit I feel like it was a boy. So for a couple of years after leaving college, I wrestled with the weight of guilt from the abortion. I finally went to talk to a priest at St. Augustine's, which is the church affiliated with University of Miami.

I had been raised Catholic, and I remembered going to the confessional as an altar boy, and it was always in two small rooms with a dark screen between them. It was weird. It made me nervous. But with this priest, it was cool. He had chairs set up in a room, and we sat down face-to-face. I told him, "You know, this thing's really weighing me down. I think I'm a murderer."

In a nutshell, he said, "Look, this is sin. And the stain of any sin, no matter how big or how small, still leaves a stain, therefore making us imperfect. The sin separates us from God and requires His forgiveness—and that's why Christ died for you. The fact that you've confessed it, the fact that you've repented of it, means you are forgiven."

I left there with a huge, weighted backpack of guilt and shame lifted off my back.

Another priest might have handled it differently. One of my best friends from childhood won't step foot in a Catholic church anymore because of the way he was treated when he sought forgiveness. Certain churches and church leaders seem more focused on beating people down than lifting them up. But this priest was great. He helped me. And I finally had that weight off my shoulders when I met Grace.

So we started jogging together and biking together, and then finally we're out to dinner, on Lincoln Road—

GRACE: I could tell he liked me, and I thought, "Ah, yikes, this isn't gonna work out." So at dinner I said, "I have to tell you something, and you're probably not gonna wanna pursue this relationship. And that's okay. I just want to make sure we stay friends because you're a great guy."

And I told him, "I'm HIV positive."

I expected him to run.

J.C.: I remember saying to myself, "All right. Wow. Okay." But if she would have told me she had cancer or diabetes or some other incurable thing, I would have said to myself, "Eh, I still wanna pursue her." And that's exactly what my response was to her telling me she had HIV.

GRACE: I still can't believe he didn't run. I remember thinking, "What guy in his right mind would want to be with me?" But he ended up breaking up with his girlfriend and going out with the one who had HIV and could potentially infect him.

J.C.: I had already been through so much. I wasn't gonna let fear stop me. Maybe I was naive, but I had already made up my mind that I would go all out to pursue her, and I did. And then, lo and behold, what happens? She gets pregnant.

GRACE: I had never been pregnant before, which was a miracle in itself.

J.C.: You had never dated a Cuban before.

GRACE: Stud.

This conversation between my parents actually happened. In front of me. Please pray for healing; I'm still recovering.

J.C.: Ha! So anyway, when we found out she was pregnant, that's when the reality of her HIV set in. Now I replayed the whole thing I went through with my first wife, thinking, "Oh no, I really am Dr. Death now because she's gonna die, and I'm gonna go get tested and find out I have the virus, and then the baby's going to have the virus . . ." I couldn't stop thinking about it. It played over and over in my head until finally I felt I was in a wrestling match with God. The voice on my left shoulder was telling me, "Abort the child and then run. Don't worry about it. God forgave you the first time. He'll forgive you again." But the voice on the other side was telling me, "J.C., for the first time in your life, do the right thing." The voice said it three times clearly. "For the first time in your life, do the right thing. Do the right thing. Do the right thing."

Then that same voice, the one on my right side, said something I could not ignore: "Just know that if you kill this child," the voice said, "I will surely let you die."

To me, that meant God would abandon me. That God would take his hand of protection off of me. That I would be left to fend for myself in the world of the enemy. It terrified me.

I listened to that voice and did the "right thing."

Grace was three months pregnant when we got married, on December 31, 1992, New Year's Eve. I was so nervous and upset about it all, I got drunk to the point of throwing up before 11:30 p.m.

Look, just because you're moving forward in faith

doesn't mean it's easy. I listened to the voice of God, but I was still stumbling around in the dark.

Even the doctors weren't sure what might happen. There hadn't been many babies born to HIV-positive mothers, so they were still learning. But once we made it clear that we weren't going to abort, one doctor told us there were three things that could happen with our baby. One, the baby would be born HIV negative, but the virus could be there, hiding out. And after two years, when the baby's immune system really kicked in, the virus might appear.

The next thing that could happen is the baby would be born HIV positive, and then at two years old, when the immune system kicked in, the virus might go away. They had observed this. It's called "seroconversion."

The third thing that might happen was our baby would be born with the virus, start getting symptoms when he or she was young, and then might not last long as a kid. Our child would die.

So I said to Grace after that meeting, "Why would we do all this testing? If what the doctor says is true, what are we going to do? Get a false negative and rejoice early? That would be stupid. And then suddenly after two years, the thing shows up and we're all devastated? We'd be better off waiting until we could know for sure."

GRACE: That's why we decided not to test until after Claudio was two. But then Gabriel came along, and they're only fifteen months apart, so we decided to wait until they were both over two and test them together.

J.C.: That was two and a half years of turmoil, real mental wrestling. "Man, how is this going to turn out?" I was so afraid. We needed guidance, and since both of us had been growing in our faith, we decided to start going to church together.

At first my parents had a hard time finding a church they liked, and my dad struggled to take the Bible seriously. I'll share more about that in upcoming chapters because I think it's important to know that faith isn't some sort of switch that flips and you suddenly understand everything about God. My parents, though they understood in their hearts and experienced God on an emotional level, they were still learning what it means to follow Him. By the time they had my brother and me, they both felt the presence of God in their lives and felt more blessed than ever that they had found each other.

GRACE: So I had Claudio, and fifteen months later, I had Gabby. Once Gabby was two and a half, we had them both tested—and neither of them tested positive for HIV.

We cried tears of joy. Both J.C. and me.

We tested them again a couple of years later, and again a couple of years after that, just to be sure. They never knew what we were testing them for. It just was part of their routine checkups. And each test came back negative. So when Claudio was seven or eight years old, we told him about my diagnosis. We waited until Gabby was ten, just because he was a little more emotional and we worried how he would take it. But he seemed to take it just fine. Thankfully there were new medicines in place by then, so it was easier to talk about, knowing for sure that my own health was going to be okay.

By that time, I had four healthy children and the miracle of my own life to be thankful for. I was already well past the ten years the doctors had told me I had left to live. So none of it was sad. It was all incredible and positive.

Not long before I started working on this book, I happened to watch the movie *Dallas Buyers Club*, the 2013 film in which Matthew McConaughey plays an AIDS patient in the mid-1980s, before any pharmaceutical treatments for the disease were approved or legally available. For the first time, that film made me realize how awful a diagnosis of HIV could be. My mom was so positive about it and stayed so healthy that I never knew how terrified she must have been when she first found out. And it really sunk in how much courage God gave her to face it down and move forward with hope, not to mention the courage God gave to my father. To love someone so much that he would risk his own health, knowing he could have caught HIV from her? It blows my mind.

They made choices: to believe in each other, to believe in themselves, to change their formerly troubled lives for the better, and most importantly to trust God with the entire process and the health of their babies. And the choices they made had a multigenerational impact, setting the stage for my own story.

It's more than that, though.

According to everything medical science had to offer at that time, the probability of me contracting HIV from my mom during the birthing process was significant. Even now, when we know the virus isn't transmitted directly from mother to child, a baby comes in contact with all sorts of bodily fluids during birth. They often *ingest* bodily fluids. So for neither me nor my older brother to be infected back then defies all odds. Both my younger sister, Sofia, and our youngest brother, Nico (who were born in 2001 and 2003) tested negative too, but they both benefitted from medications developed in the interim years, which helped prevent the transfer of infection during birth. Those medications weren't available when I was born, which really only means one thing to me—and I'm not talking about "luck."

Discovering that my health, and my very life, was a miracle helped me see the gift of life with more clarity. Knowing that my own life could have been cut short—really short—makes me realize how fortunate I am just to be walking around. Growing up, especially in my teen years, I became aware of how our decisions can change our lives. Our decisions have consequences, whether good or bad. We reap what we sow. I believe God will forgive us, and nothing can change that, but we still have to live with the outcomes of our choices. My mother's whole life changed in an instant because of her choices, and her diagnosis made me a lot more thoughtful about what I did from day to day.

Knowing my life was a miracle, I didn't want to do anything to jeopardize it.

Here's the thing, though: *Your life is a miracle too.*

Your parents' stories and the circumstances of your birth might not have been as dramatic as mine, or maybe they were *more* dramatic than mine. It doesn't change the outcome: a million things had to go right for you to be born, and a million things had to go right for you to still be alive today. None of us should take that for granted. Life is precious. It's a gift. You're *here*. You're *alive.* You have purpose. You have choices to make. You have the world at your fingertips. I know it doesn't always feel that way, but it's true. You can decide to change things for the better; it's up to you. That's what my parents did!

I know that's a lot. It's pretty heavy stuff. But I hope you'll take a minute to let it all sink in, and then ask yourself what I began asking myself at a pretty young age:

What are you going to do with this
miracle you've been given?

THREE

The Choice
Is Ours

I want to be in a *Pirates of the Caribbean* movie!"

My mom didn't know what to do with that announcement of mine. She probably laughed a little and thought I was cute. But I meant it.

I loved the *Pirates of the Caribbean* films. The first one came out when I was eight, and I thought it was just about the most exciting thing I'd ever seen. For my parents' generation it was the original *Star Wars* trilogy and the *Indiana Jones* movies and James Bond movies and other big adventure films that caught their imagination. But for me? This was one of the first big action-adventure movies I had ever seen. And while other kids liked it and wanted their parents to buy them action figures, I really, *really* wanted to be *in it*.

Watching TV and movies, seeing actors and singers and dancers do their thing, I always thought, "I can do that! I can do everything they're doing!" I didn't necessarily think I could sing like Justin Bieber. It wasn't an ego thing. For whatever reason, something inside me just knew I could act. I knew I had it in me to do what the people on the screen were doing. I could pretend, I could dance a little, I could sing a little, and I loved the idea of being on camera, and maybe behind the camera too.

I dreamed about going to Los Angeles someday, to the big city where everything in the movie and TV world seemed to happen.

When my mom got a flip phone with a built-in camera, which was like one whole megapixel of blur, I borrowed it from her and took the most jaw-dropping shots you've ever seen a prepubescent take. They were terrible. But I loved it. And one Christmas my parents bought me a little red digital camera that could . . . wait for it . . . record video! I tried to make little movies and videos with it. I opened Windows Movie Maker on the computer and tried to teach myself how to edit. I also had a friend, Timmy, who knew the program a bit and taught me some of the ins and outs of the software. But neither of my parents worked in a creative field. My mom had dabbled in modeling in Miami when she was younger, and my dad knew how to play guitar and sing, but they didn't know how to foster that growth in me. A career in the movies or TV seemed so foreign to them, so far from anything they had ever known, that it wasn't even a legitimate option. It was like I was wishing to become an astronaut and fly to Mars or something. So my early wishes weren't taken all that seriously.

What my dad really enjoyed was pushing me and Claudio to be the best wrestlers we could be. And not the WWE stuff you see on TV where they're dressed up in crazy costumes and makeup. This was the serious, real sport of wrestling, where we wore leotards (they're actually called singlets, but your boy can make a joke, lol!). So that's where we spent most of our time and effort when it came to extracurricular activities. I wrestled from age six to sixteen, starting in first grade at Calvary Christian Academy. Imagine me, the overly emotional, creatively wired little six-year-old, going out on a mat and grappling with another kid. My dad had never wrestled, but he thought it was the coolest thing that his boys got into it. He noticed right away that it took a lot of self-discipline. It required mental resilience and dedication to the craft. He was sure wrestling taught us many great values, more than most sports could teach. And it did. If we lost, he made sure we understood it was nobody's fault but our own. We didn't have teammates to blame; it was all on us. And if we wanted to succeed, that was on us as well. It was up to us to develop our own skill. But I struggled with wrestling from the start. At my first tournament, I'm pretty sure I cried walking out onto the mat. I had been wrestling only for a month or two, and I was so scared to go out in front of all the people in that huge gymnasium. Mostly I was afraid to wrestle some kid and essentially try to manhandle another six-year-old who was trying to manhandle me. I mean, how embarrassing if I lost, right? My dad had to talk me through it. He got down on his knees and grabbed hold of my shoulders and said, "Now look, Gabby. You can do this. You don't have an option; you have to do this. We don't quit in this family."

I listened to him, and I went through with it, and I won! Well, apparently. My dad claims to this day that I won, but his bias is probably just swaying his memory. I don't even remember if I won or lost. I clearly tried to suppress that memory (jokes, guys, jokes). I kept wrestling after that, even when my mother pulled Claudio and me out of school and started homeschooling the two of us full-time.

● ● ●

Making the switch to homeschooling was yet another life-altering decision our parents made that changed the trajectory of our lives.

Thanks to the COVID-19 lockdowns in 2020, a lot more families in the US got a little taste of what it's like to learn and teach at home. So give my mother the respect she deserves! My mom started just a wee twenty years earlier, without a global crisis prompting the change. She felt like the public schools in Miami had let her down when she was in school, so taking ownership of her children's education was super important to her. She didn't want to send us off in the morning and let someone else be in charge of what we thought about for seven or eight hours every day.

My mom's thought process was, "What am I unintentionally teaching my kids by not being intentional about what I'm teaching them?"

She didn't want school to be a babysitter while she worked some other job. She felt it was her job, as a parent, to stay directly involved in our education. My dad supported that, and we loved it.

My mom did a lot of research to find the best curriculum, and she ordered books tailored to that program. We went to school at the kitchen table from eight or nine in the morning till noon every day. Legit, that was it most days. We were able to cover every subject we needed, using our study time far more efficiently, in under four hours a day.

That left us with a lot of free time to pursue other things, including playing instruments and drawing—two things I loved and took to right away. I took drum lessons and taught myself other instruments while I waited for friends to get out of school and come home on the bus. People get the wrong impression that homeschool kids don't get enough social interaction, but that wasn't true at all. I felt like I had more of a social life than some of my friends who went to school full-time. While they were stuck doing homework, we were free to go bowling on a Monday with our homeschool friends, or whatever it was; the time I had with friends during weekdays was time spent playing and having fun rather than being cooped up in a classroom.

It was sad to me to have to wait so long for other kids to get home from school and then to have to wait for them some more or not see them at all because they had hours of homework to do. To be clear, my mom was not a trained teacher, but we were genuinely able to learn everything the other kids did—and then some—in less than half the time it took them, just because our lessons were so effective and intentional. And maybe that had something to do with being taught by a woman who was feeding us the sort of love and care that only a mom can give.

You know what else was cool? This was before social media was big, which meant we had a few hours to fill every day. If my brother and I didn't find something to do, we sometimes got *bored*. (Can you imagine? A world where we don't have a phone to pacify our boredom.) Many of us don't give ourselves time to think now. We're constantly distracted, knowingly or unknowingly. We immediately pick up our phones during any downtime. We almost never just sit and think, "What should I do?" Back then, Claudio and I would go outside, run around, kick a ball—a far cry from being fed information and bombarded by the constant stimulation we get from social media. They say that the cure for boredom is curiosity, and it's true! We *need* time to think, to wrestle with our own thoughts, with our own instincts and creativity. I started drawing because I was bored, and I loved it, and I got pretty good at it all on my own. I got to explore new interests and talents all because I was bored.

Boredom is powerful.

Boredom is a motivator!

I already mentioned that Claudio and I kept wrestling after we started homeschooling, but we played other sports too. For a while we participated in a physical education program for homeschoolers where a group of us would go to a park and play kickball or other sports. I loved basketball. One year I played in a city league and also at Calvary Christian Academy (the school we were still wrestling for). I probably would have pursued it if my dad hadn't made me stick to wrestling. Not to brag or anything, but I was, like, really good when I was eight years old. I know I'm joking here, but I did have a knack for basketball. Dad was fine with us playing other sports, but he wanted us to keep our commitment to wrestling, and that was during the same season as basketball every year. So it got to a point where I couldn't do both.

Wrestling exposed us to all kinds of kids from all different areas, which means we weren't sheltered in our little Christian homeschool world. You could say we were "protected" to the extent that was healthy, but we got our fair share of exposure to the outside world. We'd go to wrestling camps and hear young kids from other areas dropping f-bombs and all other sorts of words our homeschool brains took longer to process.

As we got older, just as I was entering middle school, my mom sought out a homeschooling community that could add some expertise and experience that she couldn't provide. And she found one. Through this co-op, my brother and I joined other homeschoolers in the area to get not only a more advanced education one day a week but also all kinds of experience in art, music, and more. It was kind of like an intense day full of classes, like you'd experience in college or something. It happened on Thursdays, and it was organized by a bunch of moms of other homeschool kids. (There are groups like this all over the country.) One of the moms was a trained math professor, so she took on all the math-related subjects, from algebra to calculus. One of them was trained in critical thinking and taught that. And when there were subjects they weren't experts in, they would hire other professors to come in and teach us.

This homeschool co-op pulled in kids who were from different backgrounds and from different towns and who went to different churches, but remarkably most of us shared similar values—the sorts of values my parents were trying to instill in us, like living prayerfully and looking to the Bible to guide our decisions.

Claudio and I made many friends there, friends we're still close with to this day. And contrary to what you're probably thinking, the cliques and stereotypes were similar to those in a "normal" school. There were jocks and popular kids and nerdy kids and all the rest. They would invite us over after school, and we'd do all the things that young dudes do: play video games, longboard around the neighborhood together, throw a football, pelt each other in the head with the football—you know, usual boy things. But then at dinner every once in a while, Isaac's dad, who was a football coach, would always say, "We'd love to know how you all's relationship with God is going." And we'd be expected to respond. It happened so routinely that I felt like I had to think about it before we got there. And even if I didn't have a genuine answer, I'd prepare something good to say so I sounded super spiritual. Probably not the best move on my part, but I didn't want to let the coach down. Just that little prompt from another parent made me pay attention: "Yeah. How *is* my relationship with God?"

Other parents weren't as direct, but if we put on a movie we shouldn't have been watching—like a horror movie leaning toward the demonic side of the genre (this actually happened)—they would call us out on it and ask us about it. They'd explain how these types of things could affect our hearts and minds. They held us accountable.

All these other kids' parents supported us, wanted the best for us, and wanted to see us succeed. It was the coolest thing, especially as we got into high school. If we had gone to a regular high school, the biggest influence in our lives might have been whatever we were learning from other teenagers, which I'm pretty sure isn't the best idea. Teenagers aren't prone to look out for the interests of others—or sometimes even their own! Instead, we got to learn directly from our mom every Monday through Wednesday and the homeschool co-op on Thursdays. Then, once I was about fourteen, I joined a theater program that was all day on Fridays with a bunch of other homeschool kids. That changed everything.

For a while I looked at musical theater and theater in general and thought it was kind of lame. It wasn't the movies, that's for sure. But my brother did a show the year before I did, and I could tell how much fun it was, so I decided to give it a try.

I swear, as soon as I got on stage, it's like a switch turned on. I felt alive. I *loved* it.

One of the homeschool moms was a talented theater teacher, and she ran the whole program herself. Every Friday was a full day, which meant we got to experience in one day what kids in high school might get by rehearsing every day after school for an hour at a time. Instead of spreading it out, we had one intense session each week, and I loved that intensity. The first year we did a production of *Beauty and the Beast*, and I was just a background character: I played a fork in one scene and a townsperson in another. But hearing the applause of all the parents and friends in that seven-hundred-seat theater blew my mind. The next year I tried harder and was cast as the Scarecrow in *The Wizard of* Oz. (Since I was homeschooled, this was the perfect part for me, obviously . . . because of my nonexistent brain. Ha ha!) And the next year I played the Artful Dodger in *Oliver,* which meant I was on my way to play the lead in the next show. I was confident I had the chops for it.

Being in theater was so different from participating in sports. Sports involved a super physical aspect of learning, pushing your body to the limit, ignoring the pain to achieve something. But theater involved the creative, artistic focus of trying to pull off a great performance, which was way more nerve-wracking than most sports. In a performance, if you mess up, it's not because another player was better than you; it's *you* who messed up, which went right back to what my dad was trying to teach us through wrestling. But the lesson was stronger in theater because in theater you can't blame any errors on your opponent being better than you or being the state champ or whatever excuse you could come up with. Forgetting your lines or missing steps in a dance or, the worst one, cracking during your solo—that's all on you! Being on stage is about becoming comfortable with yourself, not unlike giving a speech in front of people or doing a presentation at work; a performance is an entirely different psychological battle than sports. And I had so much fun.

I was still wrestling when I got into theater, up until I was sixteen. That year I ended up winning districts. I made it to regionals—one match away from making it to state—but my heart wasn't in it. I told my dad, and he said he understood, and he finally let me hang up the leotard. The reason I think he was okay with me stepping away from wrestling after that year was because Claudio was graduating homeschool . . . I mean high school! That meant we both graduated from our wrestling journey together that year, the journey we started a whole decade before. Dad also saw how much passion I had for theater and the arts in general, and he agreed I should follow that.

When it came time for our next show, *Tom Sawyer,* I wasn't cast in the lead role. I was cast as one of Tom's friends, which was a minor part. I couldn't understand it. "Why wouldn't she give me the lead?" I wondered. "Everyone in the cast thinks I should've had it. It makes no sense."

I didn't speak up. I didn't complain. I just worked a little harder. I thought, "I'll show her. I will just outshine him as this other character." I was sure I'd be able to redeem myself the next year.

But the next year, which was equivalent to my senior year of high school, we didn't do a show. Miss Sherry, our theater teacher, passed away. Cancer. It was devastating. We were all so sad. It was a year or so after that when someone told me something I never expected to hear: Miss Sherry had told them she didn't think I had "it," that *it* factor you need to make it in the industry. She didn't think I had that special thing it takes to make it professionally. I guess that made sense of why I never landed the lead role.

It was hard to hear. But I couldn't be mad at her. She was dead! I just wished I could have spoken to her about it, to understand what she saw in me, or *didn't* see in me, that made her feel that way.

By the time I heard this news, I had already achieved a bit of success in theater and modeling. My mom reached out to an agency she worked for when she was younger and took me to a few auditions in Miami. I landed a print ad for Coca-Cola, posing as a smiling member of a Latino family for ads that ran in Central and South America. (I never even saw the finished ad!) I did my first TV ad for slushies, which some of my friends saw a few times on Nickelodeon. And all on our own, my brother, our friend Timmy (remember him?), and I entered a high school competition called the Florida State Thespian Festival. We performed a funny scene from *The Complete Works of William Shakespeare (Abridged)* and won the critics' choice award, which essentially meant we were best in our category. Then the following year I and several of my theater buddies performed the song "What a Game!" from the musical *Ragtime*. (I got to choreograph this piece, which was super exciting.) Not only did we end up winning critics' choice again, but we were also the one act chosen to represent our district at the state festival. So this homeschool kid was feeling pretty cool. I was already proving to myself that I did have it.

After quitting wrestling and dedicating myself to the things

I loved, I also wound up getting into one of the most prestigious theater programs in the country. But I couldn't help but wonder, "What if I had heard Miss Sherry state her opinion of me? Would I have given up?" I don't know the answer to that question, but honestly, I'm glad I didn't hear her thoughts until later.

Just because someone thinks you don't "have it," just because one person—even an important, influential person in your life—thinks you can't do something, does *not* mean it's fact.

What I had come to believe by this point in my life is something much more empowering: If God has specific plans for your life that someone else might not see the potential in, that's probably a good sign. It means God can take you somewhere you aren't capable of going yourself, and He'll be glorified through it.

• • •

From the age of eight to fourteen, I lived in Coconut Creek, which is between Fort Lauderdale and Boca Raton, a little bit inland from Pompano Beach, in a house right next to my Uncle Tony's house, with a backyard that sloped down to a lake. We tore the fence down between the two houses so we could have one big, shared backyard to play in with our cousins. Up the street, in the biggest house on the block, was a kid named Kevin from Germany. And then in between, there was Jacob's house. His dad was a lead pastor at their church, and Jacob would end up following in his dad's footsteps. (Years later, Jacob was the friend who stood at the altar and officiated our wedding in Australia!) We had so much fun in that neighborhood. It was small enough that we could play right out in the streets, and we did. All the time. We were into roller-blading and set up street hockey goals with orange cones. We played football, soccer, and shot each other with airsoft guns as we ran through each other's backyards. My dad built a slide into the little pool we had, and we swam all the time. And we went out on the lake. We always had a blast.

Uncle Tony was like a second dad to us in some ways. He was around us all the time. And Tony was one person in my life who would legit talk to anyone and everyone about his faith. He just wanted to tell people about Jesus and what Jesus had done for his life. And when he got sick with cancer, his faith only grew stronger. Even in his worst days I saw that. And that influenced me. (Not all influencers are on the internet, kids.)

I was fifteen when he died. He left his wife, Cristina, my aunt, with their children—Lucas at ten, Camilla at seven, and then the baby they had adopted, Belen, who was three—and I got to see the way their family was able to recover from that. His death didn't crush them. You could say they were devastated but not destroyed. They believed that God works everything out for the good of those who love Him (Romans 8:28). That type of understanding is easy in theory. It's easy to say, "Yeah, of course God will work things out. I trust him no matter what happens." But I witnessed first-hand one of the most traumatic experiences a family could ever go through and then saw them overcome through their security in Jesus. That's a totally different level. Even through Tony's death, probably the darkest point of all of their lives, their faith didn't waver. They understood that God wanted Uncle Tony to come home, though a little earlier than they would've liked, and they believed—truly believed—that they would see him again one day. They also knew God could bring good even out of something as tragic as death and that my uncle's faithfulness was now part of the story they would get to tell.

I'm honestly tearing up in a random café while writing this part of the book. Being able to speak about that story here gives

me chills. I wish everyone who's going through something so difficult could feel the security and comfort my aunt and cousins
had in Christ. Witnessing the strength of others encourages us to
be strong. And Uncle Tony and his family had faith right till the
end, including when he smiled as he gave Claudio a hug through
the passenger window of his car on the last day we ever saw him.
I hope that sharing his story encourages people who are going
through similar situations.

Losing Uncle Tony was one more experience that showed me
how precious life is and how important it is to make the most of
life while you can.

Which brings me back around to my parents again and how
grateful I am that they made sure we were raised in a way that was
a little different from the way they had been raised. The point of
everything they did was to save us some of the pain and heartbreak
they had gone through before finding each other. They consciously
shaped our family's environment to produce fruitful lives centered
on Jesus. They didn't do that just by picking the neighborhood we
lived in and then letting chance dictate who happened to go to
our school because of where we lived. They did it purposefully,
intentionally, by moving to the house next to Uncle Tony, by pulling us out of school, by not only taking us to learn at church but
also teaching us at home, and by crossing town borders to find
people to put around us who aligned with what they wanted out
of life. Instead of just letting life happen to us, they sought out
people and educational opportunities that aligned with what they
wanted for *us*, their children, and for all of us as a family. Their
vision was clear.

They didn't let a limited budget or their past ways of living get in
the way either. They just did it. My dad completely changed his job.
He went out and got a real estate license and eventually opened his

own commercial real estate company so he could support our family while my mom homeschooled. It was that important to them, so he made ends meet no matter what. The first year after starting his own company, he brought in a whole $10,000. Now, to anyone who may be still in high school or even college and hasn't started earning their own guac yet, that probably sounds like enough cash for a lifetime. I for sure thought that! But life is expensive. And to feed a family of six on that income wasn't easy. Times were tight, but they knew what the goal was and stuck to the plan.

My dad taught all four of us kids to be responsible with money too. Any money we kids got on our birthday or Christmas or whenever, we would give 10 percent to our church and save 50 percent in our own bank account. The rest we got to enjoy however we chose. He trained us to exercise our generosity and self-control muscles early, so when we entered adulthood, we already had those healthy habits engrained in the muscle memory of our brains. He knew we wouldn't learn that lesson from any school program, so he taught us himself, with real money and real stakes.

One summer when I wanted to go away to church camp, he made me go out and earn half the tuition myself. He told me, "If this is that important to you, you need to earn it. And don't go around begging for money. You gotta work for it." I picked up odd jobs doing whatever I could to earn a few dollars here and there until I earned my share. Then and only then did he chip in the other half. I got to go to camp! I felt proud that I made it happen. That lesson taught me a work ethic and the value of earning what I want in life.

Was everything my parents did perfect? No. Clearly not. They made mistakes. They didn't have a map to follow for any of this. They just figured it out as they went along, seeking advice and mentorship from the community around them. But a huge part of accomplishing what they did was this: whenever they saw something happening that they didn't like, they changed it.

Not to expose too many personal details here, but there was a point early on in their marriage when my dad was still occasionally smoking marijuana. (I hope he's not mad at me for putting this in the book!)

J.C.: No! Please. I'm not ashamed of it. I just hope sharing this story can help someone else see things a little more clearly in their own lives.

My dad had grown up thinking marijuana was no big deal. It was nothing compared to other drugs. It was a plant. It was "natural." Now, I'm not trying to start a whole marijuana debate, so humor me for the sake of the story (lol).

One day, when Claudio was just a toddler, my dad walked into his bedroom and found Claudio standing by the bed with a joint in his hand. Dad was shocked.

"Claudio! Where did you get that?" he asked.

"Right here," Claudio said, touching the nightstand. My dad was mortified.

"This smells *good*, Daddy," Claudio said, and my dad's heart just about sank through the floor.

He took that joint from Claudio's tiny hand and flushed it down the toilet.

Dad hasn't smoked another joint since. He wouldn't allow it in our home. He changed his behavior instantly for the sake of his child. For the sake of his family. He beat himself up for allowing that to happen, for not quitting sooner, for keeping drugs in the house where his children were being raised.

But here's the thing: None of us are perfect. We're human.

What my parents showed us, again and again, is that it's up to us to choose what we do and how we live, yet understanding the consequences of our choices. And when we make mistakes, we learn and adapt so as not to make the same mistakes again. They kept on trying to live a more impactful life than the one their parents led, and the one their parents before them had led. They wanted a more fulfilled life than the one they themselves had led until just before they met each other. *They showed us again and again that it was okay to change course, to choose better, to choose smarter*—for them and for us. Nothing was predetermined. They didn't have to do something the same way their parents had done it or the same way they'd always done it. They had the freedom to choose what *they* wanted from life.

Reflect

- What kind of community and environment (school, work, church, etc.) are you a part of right now? Do you enjoy it? Are you growing as a person because of this community? Does your community support you and lift you up and encourage you?
- Are you surrounded by people whose lives you want to emulate? Do those people want the best for you? If not, what steps can you take to change that?
- If the change is a complete change of environment but you're too young to make the change yourself, what can you ask of your parents or other influential adults in your life to support you in the change you're looking for?

FOUR

Second Chances

A few years after I'd left for college, after my online career was already well underway and I had a relatively robust following on Vine, a platform where people could post six-second videos, something happened to me that's symbolic of my approach to life. Well, it wasn't just one thing, it was a series of things, really. So I hope you'll indulge me for a moment as I flash forward to tell you this story.

I'm going to keep this as anonymous as possible out of respect to those involved, but it basically went like this: A girl I started working with in LA was pretty well-known. We became friends as we worked together on a few different things. Nothing romantic was going on between us, and I wasn't even sure she was someone I could see a future with, so I left the relationship at being friends.

One day we were supposed to hang out with a group of mutual friends when everyone decided to bail last minute, leaving just me and her. We hung out that evening and it was chill. We had fun. When I look back, it did resemble a first date. But homeschool me figured we were just hanging out as friends, especially since she had a recent ex-boyfriend at the time (the details were vague, but from what I knew, she was fresh out of a relationship). As we were leaving for the night, right before she got into her car, she leaned in to kiss me. (She obviously saw it as a date. Dang it.) As she leaned in, my gut instincts kicked in and I did what any self-respecting guy would do: I turned my head and dodged the kiss and didn't say a word. (Nice one, Gabriel.)

After we stood there for probably the longest five seconds of my life (and my breaking out in an immediate sweat), she tried again, as if I didn't understand what happened the first time. And I did the same exact thing. But this time I managed to say, "Uh . . . I'm sorry." (Nailed it again. Good job, Gabs.)

We finally parted ways, and it took me a while to process everything that had just happened and how poorly I handled that situation. Poor girl, she probably felt so embarrassed leaving that night. I mean, being rejected by an ex-homeschooler of all things. That had to have been a low moment for her.

Sending the girl off with quite a dent in her self-respect, I knew I needed to have a think about my reaction. I didn't want a similar situation to unfold the same way, so I needed to implement some changes. I asked myself two things: Why did I react the way I did? And in the future, how can I handle any similar situation in a way that not only stays true to my morals but also doesn't leave the girl feeling like crap?

Wouldn't you know it? Not long after that incident, something similar happened. (What are the chances? Your boy was on fire! I'm just trying to make the homeschool community proud, ha ha!) I was hanging out with another group of friends. Once the evening was over and everyone started leaving, the last people to leave were, you guessed it, me and a girl. I saw a bit more potential for a relationship with this girl, but at this point we were definitely just friends. I walked her to her car, and she seemed hesitant to get in. She just stood there, as if waiting for something (classic foreshadowing, am I right?).

So we were standing at the car, and I could tell this girl wasn't going to just leave and make my job easy, so I either had to *do* something or *say* something. I said, "Hey, by the way, I'm not going to kiss you." (Still a terrible way to start, but please, indulge me.)

"Why not?"

"I'm not going to kiss any girl who I'm not already in a relationship with."

She looked at me for a second, processing what I just said, then replied, "I really respect that."

That was an "aha" moment for me. It clicked. Not just for this unique situation but for every situation where I could potentially be pushed to compromise my morals. I knew I couldn't always rely on my gut instincts telling me to turn my head and avoid a kiss. I needed to be able to verbalize exactly what I stood for in a clear, concise manner that didn't leave any room for misunderstanding.

Before all this happened, I may have theoretically understood the "why" of setting certain boundaries in my heart (and maybe somewhere in my head, lol), but I needed to make my goals clear as day, then in turn make the path to get to those goals clear as well. Ever since I'd hit puberty, my goal had been this: I'm not going to kiss *any* girl I'm not already in a relationship with.

I spent a bit more time with this girl to see if anything promising would arise, but ultimately our paths were different, and I chose not to pursue a relationship.

So how did I come to the no-casual-kissing resolution?

The overarching foundation I try to base my decisions from is my faith, but on a practical level, much of my understanding of and thoughts about relationships came from my parents' story.

You already know they opened up to us about my mom's HIV when we were young, but as the years went on, they purposefully opened up about many other things as well. Both had dated a lot before they met. They did their fair share of sleeping around in their early days too. (Don't worry, they gave me permission to share this story.)

They both had a lot of "experience," as people like to call it, but after getting all of that experience out of their systems, they both reached a point where they felt like those casual experiences that seemed so fun at first were actually hurting their hearts. They would often warn me and Claudio and later Sofia and Nico: Don't give pieces of your heart to anyone. Those pieces of your heart won't come back. Once you give them away, they're gone. Even something as small as a kiss. Once you have that first kiss with someone, that's it. That's the person you gave your first kiss to. I wish I could've shared that with Jess, like Claudio shared with his wife. I gave my first kiss away to someone else (more on that in a minute!) and *couldn't* give that gift to Jess. Our actions reap certain outcomes. And those outcomes only become more extreme the more of ourselves we give away.

People act as if casual sex is no big deal. With so many of us obsessing about it for so much of our lives and seeing how strong a grasp it has on our culture, sex clearly is a big deal. And now seeing how important it is in my relationship with Jess, I can't help but continue to encourage others, like my parents did with me, to take care of and be responsible with this extremely important and fragile gift God has given us.

Let's pause here for a second before we continue. I want to speak to those who may be feeling down, thinking they have "done too much" or "gone too far" and there is no hope. If you're thinking that, that's a lie. If we allow Him to, God is capable of transforming our hearts and redeeming much of the garbage we've dealt with in our past. God repairs our broken hearts. He definitely healed mine. So don't give up on yourself! If you feel like it's too late so it's pointless to even try to improve your future, then you've already lost. As I continue sharing my beliefs on this delicate subject, know I speak from a place of encouragement, a place where I urge *everyone* reading this book to better themselves each day.

There is literally nothing you can do to change your past, but there is a whole heck of a lot you can do to change your future.

Comparison is something I struggle with daily, so this reminder is as much for me as for anyone else: Don't look at other people and wish you had their life or their history. The grass is always greener when comparing yourself to someone else, and you'll only feel negative about yourself. You've been dealt a specific set of cards in your life; use them to your advantage.

● ● ●

As we got into our teen years, some buddies and I in our homeschool group developed a pact that we would always treat women with respect—and always treat ourselves and our bodies with respect too. (I'd say this was due to the environment our families helped curate for us. Don't underestimate the power that your environment has on you.) We watched out for each other and called each other out if we broke away from our values. Part of our mission, every one of us, was to save ourselves for marriage and, when the time came, to look for a wife who shared those values too.

I know it may seem a bit weird for a group of young guys to think about and prepare for marriage a decade or so before it's ever gonna happen, before any of us had even met the person we might marry, but there was a reason behind it. It wasn't just a rules thing. My parents had certain rules in our house, but they weren't rules for the sake of rules; they all stemmed from a greater "why," a greater purpose. It was a matter of intentionally going after what was important in life, and my friends and I knew it was extremely important to have marriages and families where we could be the best husbands and fathers possible. We wanted to be responsible with one of the greatest callings most of us have during our time on this planet. So it just made sense to us that we needed to be thoughtful about our relationships—even as teens. The decisions you make now carry into your future. We learned to ask ourselves: Will you end up hurting someone in the future with the decisions you're making now? And is the person you'll ending up hurting the most . . . yourself?

Because our parents were open with us about their stories and the hardships and emotional pain they'd been through because of the casual relationships they'd had, my siblings and I decided we wanted to do things differently from the start. We *chose* to do things differently. I definitely messed up sometimes. I did things my brain knew I shouldn't, but my emotions felt otherwise. But from those moments, I learned. And after years of reflecting on all the wins and losses, I've learned that not fooling around with love or sex or intimacy isn't that difficult. It's just a matter of habit building. And habit building affects everything.

The habits you build now are what you'll carry into the future, whether it's your habits with relationships, friendships, work, or something else—whatever you build now will carry through. Establishing a good work ethic early makes it easier to have a good work ethic and keep a good job later. And being lazy or blowing off work now will establish a habit of blowing off work later. It only makes sense. And we all know habits are hard to break, whether it's eating too much or smoking cigarettes or picking your nose. I'm kidding, but it's true! Habits of any kind are hard to break. They're what we get used to. We do them without thinking. Are you hurting your future by doing things without thinking?

The good news is you can create good habits too. What if you integrated positive practices that became as routine as showering or brushing your teeth?

If you develop a habit of flirting with every good-looking girl who crosses your path, I guarantee you that habit will be very hard to break once you're in a relationship. And guess how your partner is going to feel about you flirting with other people when you're supposed to be committed to each other. How do you think that's gonna go?

Maybe it will be easy to stop flirting with other people at the beginning of a more serious relationship, when all you can do is think about this new person. But when life levels out a bit and your love is determined by your commitment rather than where your emotional meter is at the moment, maybe it won't be easy at all. If that instinct to flirt isn't broken, it can be dangerous. You could wind up losing one of the best things you ever had just because of a habit you developed in your teens. A habit you never chose to break.

That's what my friends and I decided to try to avoid.

But, man. Staying committed to the mission isn't always easy. The amount of self-control it takes for a guy not to ogle every good-looking girl that passes by is mind-bogglingly frustrating. (Admit it guys, most of you know what I'm talking about.)

I can tell you firsthand that being disciplined is a whole lot easier when you surround yourself with like-minded friends. You all keep each other accountable. I think that's especially necessary when you're a teenager, when your hormones are raging. I remember being really interested in girls and trying to impress them all the time, but if I ever did anything stupid, I had people to call me out on it. We weren't shaming each other or anything like that. We just created an atmosphere of accountability. A lot of kids have that with their parents: they know their parents wouldn't approve of certain behavior, and that's enough to stop them from doing things they probably shouldn't be doing. But often their peers encourage them to do the opposite of what their parents want, and that can be dangerous. But having accountability among your peers? Not wanting to look bad in front of your friends? That's *really* powerful when you're a teen and even a young adult. Peer pressure is strong. We know it is, or we wouldn't talk about it all the time, right?

What my buddies and I created was sort of a reverse peer pressure, or a reverse of how peer pressure usually works. Instead of feeling pressured to do something we ought *not* to do, we felt pressure from each other to uphold our values. And it worked pretty well! With any girls I flirted with or liked or had feelings for in high school, I wouldn't continue down a path I knew was wrong because I knew my friends would think it was wrong too.

Just to give you an idea of how serious we all took this pact, several of those friends held out so long that their first kiss happened with the girl they're now married to. I don't fall into that category, and none of us hit the mark one hundred percent of the time, but we did the best with what we had. And today we all still feel good about the decision to respect women and ourselves and to hold each other accountable.

I've said this earlier: "Show me your friends and I'll show you your future." I think that's true, and the Bible backs it up in Proverbs 13:20 (ESV): "Whoever walks with the wise becomes wise, but the companion of fools will suffer harm."

We tend to become like the people we hang around with. If you continue to hang around people who don't act the way you want to act, you'll start acting like them. It's just human nature. We want to fit into our environment.

So how do you break free? Find people who align with the kind of person you want to be, and hang out with them instead. If you want to be more Christlike, find a community—a church, a youth group, a men's or women's group, or whatever—where you can make friends with people who have the same goals as you. If you want a healthy relationship and marriage, find other couples who want that for themselves too and who live the way you want to live. These couples can give advice, be role models, and offer you support when you struggle. Whatever it is you're aiming for, finding a community with some built-in accountability will make it a whole lot easier. I have multiple people at the ready who I can call without warning and who *want* to help me work through my struggles and be a better husband, a better Christian, a better entrepreneur, a better creative, a better friend, a better whatever; friends and family who want to see me strive to continuously improve myself, just as they want to work to improve themselves too.

• • •

Have you heard of "environment hacking," where you change your environment to benefit the goals you want to achieve? Maybe I made up that term, but I like it, and it's based on the idea of "environment design," which comes from James Clear's bestselling book *Atomic Habits*. It can refer to a change as obvious as moving to Hollywood if you want to work in the movie business. But I think choosing your friends and your community is a bigger part of environment hacking than any physical move you could ever make. Choose wisely, and the benefits will be clear. But as you choose whatever environment it is you're aiming to hack, remember, it's not all about you. No matter what community you place yourself in, you can't just be a taker. You need to contribute to that community too, or it won't work. Be a giver. Ask yourself what you can contribute, not just what you can gain.

For me, once I left for college, I had to relearn some of this community stuff the hard way. For example, my first kiss happened while I was at Florida State University, with a girl I thought I loved and who I thought loved me too. And I can't help but wonder, "If I'd had my community around me, would things have turned out differently?"

Florida State University was far enough away that I didn't hang out with anyone from home except when I went back during holidays. During that year away I wasn't as intentional as I should've been with that community back home, and as far as local community goes, I was starting from the ground up. While I should've invested in relationships and a community of people with like-minded goals there at school, I instead invested most of my emotional energy into only one relationship.

Unfortunately, I ignored some red flags in that first relationship (maybe because I didn't recognize them as red flags) and learned some hard lessons because of it, so I guess I'll go ahead and tell you about those here too.

● ● ●

I met her at Dunkin' Donuts during move-in weekend. She was there with her little sister, and they recognized me from my Vines. She asked if I could take a photo with her sister, so I did. I remember thinking this girl was really pretty (the older one, not the little sister!).

We ended up messaging back and forth a little and decided to hang out in person only a few days later. We met up and ate at a restaurant on campus. That's when she let me know she had a boyfriend. They had been together for two years, in high school, and now he was going to school in New York. It was the first time they had been apart, she told me, and they were having "problems."

When she mentioned she had a boyfriend, half of me decided, "Okay, a relationship obviously isn't an option," but the other half of me felt that if I stayed "friends" with her and she broke up with her boyfriend, I'd be right there, willing, ready, and able. If my boys were there, they would have said, "Hey, you know how stupid that is, right?" But there I was, with only my emotions to talk to, and they were very convincing.

Over the next few weeks, I continued to spend time with her here and there, just as friends, but we were opening up, getting to know each other and getting closer emotionally. I believe neither of us had any malicious intent and genuinely thought we could be friends. But I was not respecting her current relationship, spending one-on-one time together with her while she still had a boyfriend.

They continued to have problems dealing with the distance, and I never knew if my presence was hurting their preexisting issues, but in retrospect, I can say with confidence, I obviously didn't help *at all*.

One day she called me crying. She and her boyfriend had broken up. She came to me so upset and told me all about it. She ran to me, a guy she clearly had feelings for and who clearly had feelings for her, and poured her heart out to me just fifteen minutes after a breakup with another guy. And I didn't even try to stop it. That should've been a red flag right there—I shouldn't have been the guy she was comfortable going to about her breakup. She should've been with friends, given space to heal outside of any relationship, but I was selfish and let myself be that guy.

Anyways, our relationship began in not the smartest way, but here we were. Before I knew it, we were spending all our free time together.

We would meet up at Landis Green, the big green field in the middle of campus, before going to the cafeteria and grabbing lunch together. I met her roommates and her classmates, and we talked about *everything*. I was open and up front about how I wanted a relationship to go, that I wasn't interested in something short-term. My goal was marriage. She lit up when I said that. She seemed to love that idea.

We went to Cru together, the Christian group on campus. And we read the Bible together at times. That was important to me. I thought, "Is this someone I could spend the rest of my life with?" But in hindsight, our relationship didn't start from this place of faith. Its foundations were not nearly as pretty.

I fell for her, completely. I went all in. She was my first kiss. I was in love for the first time ever, and it was overwhelming and emotionally consuming. I went over the top after all that waiting. I wanted to be with her all the time. I wanted to do everything with her.

The only thing that seemed a little weird was that her ex would occasionally check up on her. And she would answer him. And then she would check up on *him*. I remember thinking, "You know, that's not helping either of you to move on."

I wondered why she would do that when it clearly made me uncomfortable. I wanted to know that the commitment to the relationship was equal on both sides. In all my actions the only thing I wanted to show her was that the only person who had my heart, the only person I wanted to focus on, was her. I didn't want anything to get in the way of her knowing how important this relationship was to me, and I definitely didn't want to do anything to hurt her. (Ironically, at this point, I already had—by hanging out with her so much, and therefore disrespecting her and her relationship—even though I didn't realize it yet.)

I tried to be cool. I tried not to overthink it. I rationalized what she was doing by assuming it was taking her a little time to get over him, which sort of made sense to me. So I pushed my worry aside.

Then I saw something on Snapchat that I thought was a little weird too.

If you were on Snapchat way back when, you might remember this, or not, but you used to be able to see everybody's top three "best friends" listed on their profile. We had been dating for about two months at that point, when I noticed that the #2 and #3 friends that showed up on her profile were friends of hers that I recognized, but the #1 friend was a random username I didn't recognize. So I asked her who it was. And it was *him*.

"So you're talking to him all the time?" I asked her.

"No, not *all* the time," she said. "But . . . well, he was my best friend for two years. That doesn't go away easily, you know?"

That hurt.

We continued this conversation a few more times after this incident, which lifted tensions between us a bit. But this all happened right before Thanksgiving break, and things felt uneasy when we said goodbye for the long week away from school.

I didn't have a car then, and she lived about an hour north of my parents' place. So we didn't get to see each other over the break, which made things even worse when she told me that her mom had invited her ex to come visit.

"What?" I asked.

Apparently, her mom was "really attached to him," she said.

Part of me was glad she told me. She was open with me. She didn't lie to me. That was good. But it wasn't comforting. The whole thing felt off to me.

And then, because she "didn't want to hide anything from

me," she told me that when she walked him out to his car to say goodbye, he had *kissed her*!

My stomach tied up in a knot like I'd never felt before.

We got back to school with only a couple of weeks left of classes and finals before we left for winter break, and my head kept spinning the whole time. I finally let it all out and asked her everything: "What the heck is going on? Why would your mom invite him over? And did you . . . did you kiss him *back*?"

I honestly don't remember what most of her answers were.

I was filled with all these terrible feelings, a jealousy and insecurity that made me feel sick inside. I had given my heart to this girl.

"No!" she insisted. "You can trust me."

I calmed down a bit.

"I don't want to mess this up," I told her.

But something still felt off.

She mentioned that she wanted a little break from texting all the time during those weeks apart between semesters. She needed some space to think about everything, I guess.

I did everything I could not to lose my mind during those three weeks. I focused on posting a bunch of Vines and turned my attention to YouTube too, finally posting consistent videos each week. But right before the break ended, she posted on her Snapchat story that she was in South Beach on vacation.

She hadn't mentioned anything about going to South Beach.

South Beach is in Miami, which is south of my parents' house. She basically had to drive right past me to get there. *Why wouldn't she have stopped in to say hey? Or at least* mentioned *it?*

I figured she was with her family, but I had a bad feeling something was up.

So did my mom. She was there watching me that entire Christmas break and saw some of the drama I was dealing with. "This isn't healthy," she said.

My mom, per usual, was right. And I knew it too. It wasn't what I wanted to hear because I wanted this relationship to work out so badly, but it was what I needed to hear from someone who had my best interests at heart.

Back to the girl. I didn't want to get in a fight over the phone, so the day we got back to campus at the start of the new year, I asked about her trip. I knew she wouldn't lie to me, so I started asking questions.

"Were you there with your family?"

"No."

"Friends?"

"No."

I took a deep breath. "Were you there with *him*?"

She looked down at the table, like a little kid who'd been caught stealing or something. "Yeah," she said, "I was."

I could feel my blood boiling. We were sitting in a little café when she told me. It was super quiet, with people studying all around us. Unable to fully compose myself, I grabbed my backpack and stormed out. Pretty sure I wasn't too subtle in that quiet café. But I left. It was over. I couldn't do this anymore. This was not the kind of relationship I wanted to be in. I couldn't understand how it could possibly be the sort of relationship she wanted to be in either. Or that anyone would want to be in. If she wanted out, why didn't she just break up with me?

Regardless, I was *done*.

She tried to reach out to me several times after that. We had signed up for a class together—a class on Old Testament studies, funny enough—so at least once a week, sometimes twice, I sat in the same small classroom with her. And on occasion she would text me questions about homework and whatnot, but from my end, I was moving on.

The last time she reached out was that summer, after I had left school and moved to LA. I never responded to that last text. And not long after, I had to get a new phone number, and I never gave it to her. It wasn't out of spite; I genuinely wanted to respond and see how she was doing, but I knew it was best to keep that chapter of my life closed. And I knew that when I eventually met the next person I would begin a relationship with that having ended communication with my ex would automatically introduce trust into the relationship.

I suppose a lot of people's first relationships aren't perfect. But it was really hard for me. I had waited so long because I wanted to do things right, only to screw up and get my heart broken—and then to leave that relationship with a whole lot of trust issues.

I beat myself up for falling too hard too fast. But I found relief in the fact that I had the future to look forward to and a new store of knowledge to help me make better decisions moving forward. I could identify some of the red flags that could pop up since I now understood what to look for and what not to replicate in my next relationship.

In the end, it was simple: We didn't see eye to eye on some important things. Our values weren't aligned. It seemed like they were in the beginning, but they weren't. Or at least the most important values weren't.

I'm an all-in kind of person. When I want something, I don't just sit around and wait for it to happen, I make it happen. So I guess it makes sense that my falling in love for the first time had a certain speed and intensity to it. Going all in was good for most areas of my life, but clearly this time I should've been more cautious. The whole relationship played out really fast. It was over within one semester, and because of that, some people I've shared this story with have diminished what happened. Maybe you too think it doesn't sound like that big of a deal. But even though it happened quickly, it was a powerful, serious experience of first love, and painful loss.

I steered clear of dating that whole next year.

I was still keeping clear of it when I left school early to move to LA and pursue my career.

The next could've-turned-romantic encounter I had with a girl was the one I talked about at the beginning of this chapter: the girl who tried to kiss me, with the ex-boyfriend. (I guess my first relationship explains a little better why I reacted the way I did. Though royally embarrassing myself, I knew what I wouldn't compromise on.) The whole situation looked awfully familiar, with the whole fresh ex situation, so I understood what *not* to do.

After everything went downhill with my ex, I didn't shut myself off from the world and just wait for love to come find me. I opened up a bit after I got to LA. I took some time to try to get to know a few people, to see if there might be a future with them. But I was specific with what I was looking for now, so nothing stuck. I recognized the differences in values and noticed any red flags, whether in how they acted, in the stories they told me about other guys they'd dated, how they spoke about their faith, whatever. So I didn't move forward with any of them. I knew what I wanted, and I trusted that I would find it. Or that it would find me. And this time, in LA, I sought out likeminded people of faith who I could do life with and find support in. I neglected that at FSU and had paid the price.

To this day, I meet with friends once or twice a month to discuss what's going on in our hearts and minds, in our relationships, and in our marriages. These get togethers are with my local friends here in Florida, where I currently live. But even with the close friends I made in LA, I still talk with them weekly, whether over text or on FaceTime. We keep each other up to date and support each other with the deep and important parts of our lives that we all want to see flourish.

Not to get too far ahead of myself, but here's the magic of that kind of support system: If it *weren't* for these friends, and the environment I was in, to help keep me on track, I might never have been in a position to marry Jess—because Jess wouldn't have married *me*.

Even though she was raised under different circumstances, by different parents, in a different church, with different friends, on the other side of the *world*, she was looking for the same thing I was looking for. And God made it happen. Being patient, being intentional with what we wanted in a partner, led each of us to find the other.

Everything I'm sharing is obviously from my own experience. And from my experience, I know that because of a decision—a whole series of decisions, really—to live my life a certain way, to surround myself with people I want to be like, to shape my life off the truth of the Bible, I knew the type of guy I wanted to be. I knew how I wanted to conduct myself. The way you act is what you attract. And I don't mean that in some sort of mystical way. It just makes logical sense. Character attracts character. Jess would never have committed herself to me if I was sleeping around or wasn't serious about my faith. If she was the type of girl I wanted, I had to be the person she would want to marry.

Are you the type of person you would want to marry?

Are you honest? Are you quick to forgive? Are you quick to apologize? Are you slow to get angry? Do you always want the best for others, even when it's not in your best interest? Are you expecting someone to be sexually pure, while you yourself are doing nothing to maintain your own sexual purity?

These can be harsh questions, but they help us evaluate what changes we need to make.

It's not that complicated, is it? Doing whatever you want and messing around however you want and then flipping a switch to settle into a perfectly loving, stable relationship is almost impossible. Maybe there are examples of that happening somewhere in the world, but I haven't experienced it. The divorce rates are high enough to show that the way our society treats relationships does not lead to healthier, happier marriages.

I'm not here to say I know everything about relationships, because I don't. There are people out there much wiser and who have much more experience than my five years of marriage. But I do know this: Jess and I are so committed to our relationship that we choose to learn and adapt to make the most out of this gift of marriage God has given us. And I don't plan on messing it up.

If you're unhappy about where you are in life, consider the choices that might have *led to* those results. Whether it was you or someone else who caused you to go down a road that hasn't worked out for you, go ahead and do something about it. Change!

As some anonymous genius in the past once said, "The definition of insanity is doing the same thing over and over again and expecting different results."

I understand it's not easy to change the way you live, especially if you've been living a certain way for years, or even decades. It's a lot easier to make good choices early on, to pick the right path when you a see a fork in the road. But I believe *there are many opportunities throughout life—alternate routes—to get you back on the road you want to be on. Second chances. Third chances. Fourth chances exist. Notice them.* See those forks in the road for the opportunities they are. I'm convinced God puts them there for us all the time, but most of us are driving too fast (or possibly in the wrong direction) to see the signs.

Saying no to being kissed by that girl in LA was a second fork in the road for me. It might seem silly and insignificant, but it was a defining moment for me. I'm writing about it in this book, after all. And I chose correctly that time (though painfully awkward to experience and now write down on paper), and that choice kept me on the right road.

I know some people think the choices I made seem boring. We're told again and again that we should get some "experience" while we're young; we should go out and "have fun," get things out of our system, and all kinds of other advice that I think might be the wrong advice, given how much heartache I see in the world. And maybe my choices *were* boring. But I'll tell you what, I would happily live through a few years of not being over-stimulated to get to the kind of fulfillment I have now. Especially when I think about how much heartache I saw in my parents' eyes when they described how they lived before they met each other, before they had kids, and before they had a real relationship with God.

Plus, boredom is a motivator. Even in romance! By not jumping from one relationship to the next, you give yourself time to think and look inward and explore what you really want out of your relationships.

People ask me if I ever feel like I missed out. Honestly? Yeah. I mean, I *chose* to miss out. Sometimes I wonder what my life would've been like if I had followed whatever urge or attraction I had. It's human nature to wonder, "What if?" But then I look around at those who chose the lifestyle that could have been mine, and I'm perfectly content, knowing I made the right decision.

I look at Jess and think about our life together, and I know that nothing could make me regret what I have with her.

Reflect

- Do you have a vision or goals for a relationship or your life as a whole? If you've never given it a lot of thought, take a minute and think of the person you'd like to become one day. Are you working toward that vision? Or are you working against it?
- What habits are you developing that will help you reach your goals and overall vision?
- What habits might be hurting you in that mission? And how can you change them?
- Do you have people who will hold you accountable and help you live up to your own long-term goals, despite the temptations that come in the short term? If not, what can you do to change that?

FIVE

The Existence
of Aliens

As you know by now, my faith and belief in Jesus are a huge part of what makes me who I am. And if you've followed me and Jess on social media for any amount of time, you know we don't speak about our faith or share our specific beliefs in every video or post. We simply show our life. And when the moment calls for it, we speak about Jesus.

I love the quote, "Preach the gospel at all times; when necessary, use words." (Commonly misattributed to St. Francis of Assisi.) That's the model Jess and I have adopted when it comes to our life and our presence on social media. We don't want to cram our beliefs down anyone's throat; they clearly have to decide for themselves, but we want to share our lives with others in such a way that they *know* we're followers of Jesus.

Hence my approach in writing this book. Yes, I'm a Christian, and no, I'm not worried about talking about my faith, but I believe actions speak louder than words. And that's why I'm telling the story of my life: to *show* the effect God has had on me and my family and why I live the way I do.

It's honestly quite surprising sometimes, with our being "mainstream" influencers, that some people say they started going to church because of our videos, or they started reading their Bible again. At least once a month, I think, "Why me? Why us? God, why did you give *us* this platform?" And this humility is genuine, I promise. It can sound like a load of bull, I get it. But it's all true and part of the story. God has used our platform, and I won't diminish His work, even if we are the tools He used to make it happen.

If you're not a Christian, please don't close this book here. I hope you've gotten something from these pages thus far, and I still have more to share that you can apply whether or not you believe what I believe. Of course I'd love you to believe what I believe to be true! But that's not up to me.

All I know is that my parents raised me to have a relationship with God—a relationship that they didn't develop until their late twenties—and that relationship changed their lives and mine. And that is why I aim to live out what I believe in every aspect of life.

Let me tell you about my buddy Sebastian.

I met Sebastian in 2015 at a social media convention in New York City, and in a lot of ways, the two of us could not have been more different. He was a partier. He loved going out and going crazy. The f-bomb came out of his mouth as often as the word *the*. But for some reason, we hit it off. We became friends. (If you've watched us on YouTube, you've definitely seen and heard of Sebastian. He's hard to miss!)

When we first started hanging out, he would ask why I didn't drink and especially why I didn't swear, so I'd open up about my faith and why I live the way I do.

One of the nights, we were at McDonald's, and Sebastian was talking about UFOs and asked if I thought aliens exist, which is kind of a loaded question. But of course he had to ask me; I was the "Christian" guy.

If you've seen anything of Seb, you know how genuine he is, so I knew he actually wanted my opinion and was curious. So I answered. My answer was this: God is so big that He created the entire universe, and He put us on this little, tiny, microscopic planet—at least in the scope of the universe. And He loves us enough that even after doing all of that, He sent Jesus to earth so we could have a relationship with Him. It all points back to how powerful He is and, in turn, how much He must care about us.

Maybe aliens exist; that'd be kind of cool. But from what I know now, I can't say they do. I think the universe was created like it says in the Bible, and through its creation we can see God in everything. So I told Sebastian, as of right now, I'm of the opinion that God created the entire universe for us to research and look at and observe. He made this mind-boggling, complicated, intricately detailed, interconnected world; and He did all of that essentially to say, "Look. I have done all of *this*, and I still care about *you*!"

The conversation obviously went a little longer than just that, with plenty of questions and answers back and forth, but you get the gist.

Anyway, Sebastian thought I made a pretty good point. Now, I'm not saying that discussion drastically changed his life. But it definitely planted a seed in his mind.

After that trip to New York (and after I had prematurely given my phone number to him), Sebastian would make late-night calls to me almost every weekend while sloshed at a party or club or just with some friends. He was usually drunk and always ready to chat! It would be past midnight in New York but only nine o'clock or so in LA. So I listened (and laughed).

He wasn't able to put it into words at the time, but I could tell he was seeking something.

Eventually, when he was visiting one day, he asked if he could come to church with me and Jess.

"Yeah, of course," I said. And from that point forward, he never looked back. Sebastian—kind of like my mom—found what he was looking for the whole time, the thing that filled the holes in his heart. He found some of it confusing, but, like my parents, he committed to gaining the knowledge behind what he was experiencing in his heart. He continued to develop his relationship with God, and it truly changed his life. It put him on a track that wasn't necessarily *easier* than doing whatever he wanted whenever he wanted, but it gave him a purpose for his life he had never experienced until then.

Just to show you how extreme the change in him has been, here is the Sebastian we know and love today: He is one of the most inspiring people I know. He is constantly reading and growing in his knowledge of the Bible, talks with God like God is an actual person (which is like, duh, but seeing Seb's understanding of that is amazing), is committed to sexual purity, and legit prays over every Uber driver who has the pleasure of driving him. And those are just a few examples off the top of my head. He is entirely different from who he used to be.

Not long ago, Sebastian told me a story from before I knew him, the story of his first kiss. The conversation was one of the funniest things ever, especially since I cannot imagine him doing any of what he told me. But it goes to show the change that has happened in his heart.

One night Seb was out with his friends, and he was determined to have his first kiss. Apparently, he was a "late bloomer," so he was intent on making it happen that night. I don't know the details, but he had his first kiss at some point that night with some random girl. But that's not the funny part. The funny part is that right after he had his first kiss, he immediately decided it'd be a good idea to keep going. So he set his sights high and decided to kiss as many girls as possible before the night was over. That night, the night of Sebastian's first kiss, he kissed twenty-six girls. *Twenty-six!* If that doesn't show the power of goal setting, I don't know what does.

As I was working on this chapter, I checked in with him, and he confirmed something I already knew: Since 2017, Sebastian has kissed only one girl. And even that he wasn't necessarily proud of. He hasn't found his "one" yet. But he's on his way. And he doesn't "have it all together" (none of us do, really), but he's at peace knowing God has a plan for his life. He's happier and more comfortable with himself than he was when we first met. And he's still a blast to be around. He's a nutcase, honestly! He's still the life of the party, but without having to suffer a whole lot of regret and pain and feeling bad about himself the morning after.

Who would've thought he'd end up here just from a light-hearted conversation about aliens? Well, God did.

Same with my parents. I can't even imagine my parents before they were Christians. Knowing them as I do now, it doesn't make sense, hearing the stories of what their lives were like. But my father initially struggled with the idea of letting God in.

After my mom got pregnant with Claudio and my parents married, they both struggled to find peace. They had both been through a lot of turmoil. They needed help. They needed guidance. They felt like they needed a community of spiritual people to help them through that difficult time of waiting to find out whether their babies (me included) would be born with a potentially deadly virus.

Since they both felt let down by their personal experiences with the Catholic Church, they decided to look for a church community elsewhere.

I'll let Dad tell the story:

J.C.: At first we went to North Miami Beach, to a hyper-Pentecostal church where people would get touched by the Spirit and speak in tongues and run laps around the pews. It was just about as different from a

Catholic church as you could get. Almost every time we were there, the pastor's son would stand up and shout, "We know there are fifteen people out there who have a hundred-dollar bill in their pocket!" They basically preached that if Grace and I had enough faith, we would both be healed—but if we didn't have enough faith, we might not. Like it would be all our fault if something went wrong with us or our babies. And part of showing our faith was about giving them more money. That felt manipulative after a while. They made it seem like someone getting cancer and not being cured of it was their own fault because their faith wasn't strong enough. That didn't feel right to us.

While we were at that church, and while Grace was pregnant with Gabe, I started reading the Bible again. I hadn't read any of it since I was forced to when I was a kid. I remember we were living at her parents' house because we were broke and both of us had a bunch of debt, which was another strain on us. I was somewhere in the middle of the Old Testament when it got to me. I shouted, "This is the biggest crock of crap I've ever read!"

I put my Bible down on the nightstand and went to sleep, and that night, I had a dream.

My mother died of cancer when I was sixteen years old, and I had not dreamed about my mother in the eighteen years since. But in this dream, I was in the house where I grew up, in Key Biscayne, standing back-to-back with my brother. We were doing some remodeling work in the kitchen. I turned around, and my mom was standing right there. "Mommy," I said, "what are you doing?" I grabbed hold of her arm. "What are you doing here? I've missed you like crazy."

She didn't answer.

"Hang on a second," I said. "I got a lotta questions to ask you."

I turned around and took off my tool belt and set it on the counter. When I turned back, she was gone. I looked out the window and I could see her, walking across the street toward the Catholic church where I had been an altar boy, and I ran after her, full blast. I took her arm again and said, "Mommy, where are you going?"

"No, no, no, I have things to do," she said, "but you go back and keep doing what you're doing."

To me, what she meant was, "Keep on reading the Bible." Metaphorically, she was saying she wanted me to go back and put on my tool belt and continue my project.

The Bible was my tool belt. The kitchen was the building of my faith.

So even though I didn't believe everything I read in those pages, and even though some of it still felt like a whole lot of nothing, I kept reading the Old Testament, and reading some New Testament too, until the Lord led us out of that particular church and we found a new church, which was up in Fort Lauderdale. Once we found that church, everything started to make sense. There was no manipulating for money. They placed boxes in the back of the church, and we were encouraged to give if we felt moved to do so, but it was up to us. "Jesus was a joyful giver," they said.

They taught from the Old Testament on Wednesdays and the New Testament on Sundays, and no one made us feel guilty or ashamed for anything we had done in the past. What mattered was we were there now, repentant and wanting to embrace God in our lives. They welcomed us with open arms—so much so that we decided to move closer to that church, away from Miami, as soon as we could afford to do so. We accepted Jesus into our hearts, and life has been purposeful and fulfilling ever since—it's hard to even put into words.

The two of us knew we wanted to raise our kids to develop their own relationships with God, and the church equipped us with the tools to do just that. We hoped our kids would start out on a better footing, with a better understanding than we had, so hopefully they wouldn't have to go through the sorts of tests and trials Grace and I had both gone through.

My dad is a great example of how a person can connect with God at any point in life, no matter what they've been up to or how much they resisted it in the past.

• • •

It didn't take me quite as long as my parents to accept Jesus into my life. One Sunday at church, when I was five years old, I raised my hand and prayed for Jesus to enter my heart. I remember it vividly—this snapshot of the room and actually understanding what I was doing. A lot of people don't accept Jesus until they're older, but for whatever reason, I decided to do it then.

I already knew the story of Jesus, and I understood it all enough to realize His love for me. So welcoming Him into my life was pretty seamless.

But it wasn't until early high school when I truly understood what I had been taught, seeing the depth of the Jesus story for what it was. I questioned things and dug deeper and made sense of the faith in which I'd been raised. And what's funny is, for me, studying science made God *more* real.

That's the opposite of what we usually hear, right? People act as if science and religion are on opposite ends of the spectrum. But the more I learned about how complicated yet intricately designed the world is, the more I wondered, "How could this possibly be random?"

I didn't read theology and science books in my room at fourteen years old, but I did take a few classes that bridged the gap between science and theology and took a course at my church—outside of normal Sunday sermons—that allowed me to dig a little deeper into understanding what it is I actually believe. And the older I got, the more I questioned and learned and looked for answers, trying to make sense of the world we live in.

Growing up surrounded by other kids and their parents who embraced some of these same ideas made talking about our beliefs, as well as our doubts, easy. When something terrible happened in the world and I questioned why God would allow such a thing, there was always a parent or teacher or somebody around who was willing to talk it out and share their thoughts on it too. Having that community, both in the church and in our homeschooling and peer group, made such a difference. No one stopped us from asking questions or shamed us for doubting God sometimes. We were encouraged to talk about how we felt, and that made such a difference in all of our lives.

I'll be honest, it wasn't always an open dialogue. At home, I didn't always feel like I could fully question everything without getting in trouble, especially with my dad, who so strongly wanted us to believe as he did.

Coming to faith is not easy for everyone. Some people feel forced to believe a certain way when they're young. Some have bad experiences and wind up rejecting the church altogether, and it's hard for some to ever trust in a church or pastor again. I completely understand. Jess and I have been burned several times by other Christians and people at certain churches we went to. But we were able to recognize that those issues were with people, not with God. People can really suck sometimes, and guess what? The church is full of people. Problems will arise sooner or later.

I'm incredibly thankful that I grew up with strong community around me. I feel like that support system is a huge part of what helped me flourish early in life. But you can seek that kind of support anytime you want to. Whenever you're ready. Even later in life, like my parents did. It might not be easy. You might even have to look outside your own immediate community or even your town. But it's possible.

Support matters.

Who you surround yourself with matters.

My parents came to their strong belief in God later in life and were able to start sharing that with my brothers and sister and me at the same time they were still strengthening their faith themselves.

Each generation has the opportunity to benefit and learn from the generation that came before, to carry the baton further. God works generationally. He allows us to continue growing and building our family legacies, whether that's through a change of direction (like my parents took) or by building on the foundation that has already been set, continuing what worked and adjusting what didn't.

My family's journey is too important for me to neglect. My parents weren't perfect; no parents are. But they did their best to improve upon what their parents did, and to equip me and my siblings to improve upon that. I know I have a responsibility to continue what my parents started—to be the best husband to my wife and the best father to my children, helping to grow and nurture them with our family mission in mind, so they can one day carry the torch, whatever that may look like. (You'll learn more about the Conte family mission in the last chapter!)

In reality, though, my story started even before my parents.

Reflect

> - Have you taken the time to develop a personal perspective or worldview on what you truly believe about the world you live in? And about the God you may or may not believe in? Or have you simply accepted what you've heard?
> - Are you willing to have your beliefs questioned, putting yourself in conversations with others who have different views than your own?
> - Have you reflected on your beliefs enough to know how to confidently communicate them when an opportunity presents itself?

SIX

A Family History Lesson

The older I get, the more I learn about my mother's family and my father's family—both of whom immigrated to the US just before my parents were born—and the more I recognize the paths they created and the foundations they laid for my parents to build upon. And for *me* to build upon.

My mother's father was born in Spain and grew up while Hitler's army encroached on southern Europe during World War II. But under that very real threat and all the stress and worry, which is hard for most Americans even to imagine, he had a dream: he wanted to go to America. So he went to the library whenever he could and picked up every American book he could find. He taught himself English! He took that initiative as a kid and continued learning English as a teenager.

When he went into the military, which was mandatory back then, his English was a huge leg up. Instead of starting at the bottom and working the grunt jobs many young soldiers had to endure, he was assigned to work directly for a general, translating for him and teaching him English.

When he was finally able to leave Spain on his own, my grandfather didn't make it to America right away. He took a detour to Venezuela, where his older brother had a job with an American oil company. He got a job with the oil company too but had a side hustle teaching English to families all over town. And one of the families he taught English to was my mom's mom and her family.

My grandmother's parents had just moved the family to Venezuela from Colombia to escape some of the things going on there. And Venezuela is where my grandmother and grandfather fell in love, married, and gave birth to my mom's older brother before my grandfather finally arranged to get a transfer to the oil company's headquarters—in New Orleans.

Even though my grandmother didn't speak any English, she settled into life in New Orleans while her husband worked a full-time job and simultaneously went to Tulane University to earn his degree in accounting. (What an absolute monster, lol.)

This was the 1960s, when all sorts of racial tensions gripped the South, and my grandmother, not understanding English, wasn't sure what to make of it all. She had never seen racism like that before, and she wasn't sure where she fit in. Her skin was dark brown, so she assumed people saw her as Black. She used to ride in the back of the bus so as not to cause any trouble. But one day, some white people went to the back of the bus and took her by the arm and walked her to the front. They didn't see her as Black, and she didn't realize it until that moment. True story.

It was there, in New Orleans, that my mother was born.

Once my grandfather had his degree, when my mom was only eight months old, the company moved him back to Venezuela, where they lived for the next six years or so. That's where they enrolled my mom in Catholic school. When they moved to Spain, she went to a Catholic school in Madrid too. But a year later, when things in Spain weren't working out for them, it was my grandmother who decided they should settle in America for good. And my grandfather obliged.

Can you imagine picking up and moving to different countries like that? With kids? Even when you don't speak the language? My grandma had guts. And my grandparents both worked hard to give themselves and their kids a better life than the one either of them had known.

My dad's family went through an even more dramatic trans-formation. His grandparents in Cuba were incredibly wealthy. They lived in an oceanfront mansion where they had a full-time, white-gloved staff. According to my dad, my great-grandfather, Rafael Conte, was one of the first, if not *the* first, Cubans to attend Harvard University. He wrote a book in the early 1900s and had such acclaim that the baseball stadium in Havana is actu-ally named for him: "Estadio Rafael Conte"! His daughter (my grandmother, Annie Facio Conte—my father's mother) wanted to become an architect, but Rafael didn't think it was appropriate for a woman to go to college. Still, she studied, and eventually he let her design an eight-story apartment building across the street from their home. Finding out all of this blew my mind. I had no idea there was that level of wealth in my history. And part of the reason I didn't know is because it was all taken from them.

When Fidel Castro came to power during the Cuban revo-lution of 1958, my grandparents were forced to leave everything behind. (Castro took over the apartment building my grandmother designed and used it to house his military personnel.) From what I understand of that time, they were lucky to make it to America, though with not much more than the shirts on their backs. They had no choice but to start over from scratch, and my dad, who was born soon after, was raised for his first few years in New Jersey and later Miami as they found their way all over again.

My father never knew the wealth or the lifestyle his parents once did, but he was always taught that he could build a life of his choosing, a life of his dreams.

My grandparents recovered pretty well themselves. After enduring the grief of my grandmother's early death, my grandfather became the first mayor of Key Biscayne, a little island just off the coast of Miami. He was the mayor when my mom and dad met.

I can't help but wonder if some of my entrepreneurial ethic came from his side of the family, where the entrepreneurial spirit and a serious work ethic ran thick.

It is crazy to see parts of my family's history and how certain traits and actions were handed down and somewhat replicated in my life (leaving my home, going to a "new land" to chase a dream, etc.). And most of that happened before I knew all the details of my family history. The decisions my grandparents made changed not just the direction they were headed but also the direction their *families* were headed. They shifted course in such a way that their grandchildren are now reaping the rewards of the legacy they began. Just as my parents' decisions will have a multigenerational impact on the entire Conte lineage. It's profound! And that legacy continues to point right back to God.

● ● ●

My dad took the entrepreneurial spirit he inherited and started his own commercial real estate company. Real estate is where he found his financial success, which allowed our family to grow and helped pay for our education as my brother and I headed into our college years. He found it was a profession that worked well for him, so he encouraged me to get into it too.

If I got a head start in real estate, he thought, I'd be much better off financially than he was at a young age. So right after graduation, in 2013, the summer before I started college at Florida Atlantic University (a public university located right in Boca that I attended before I transferred to Florida State University), I took a real estate course per my father's wishes.

It wasn't exactly what I wanted to do with my time, but I enrolled in the class with Claudio, so at least I had my brother with me. That made it fun. At the end of the course, I needed to score at least a seventy-five on my final exam in order to pass. Guess what I got. A seventy-three. Claudio passed, though. You know what that meant? I had to take the course again. By myself. What a drag.

One day, on the second time through the course, I was so bored that I got on my phone to curb the pain. And that's when I noticed that a new app, Vine, was available on Android. All my friends had had Vine for several months at that point, but I hadn't been able to partake in all the fun because I couldn't afford an iPhone. I was eager to make content, and now that I had access, I downloaded it right there in class. (Don't do this, kids! Pay attention in class, lol.)

If you don't remember Vine, it was a social media platform where people could shoot and post six-second videos. It was like an early, low-res, shorter version of TikTok, years before TikTok existed.

The stuff people posted on Vine was totally homemade. I found it entertaining, and the quality inspired me to do more than just watch. It seemed like such a low barrier to entry into sharing content with the world.

When I was growing up, my dad often had me work on things and toward things (for example, wrestling) that grew me in many ways. But my heart was usually elsewhere. In this case, rather than simply being a distraction, Vine led to my career in entertainment, taking me away from my father's own career path in real estate. It's funny looking back and seeing how God makes things work sometimes.

Going on Vine definitely distracted me from what I was supposed to be doing. I still needed that minimum score of seventy-five to pass the exam and get my real estate license—and this time I got a seventy-four.

Hey, at least I improved!

At that point I pulled the plug on the real estate course, but I still helped my dad with his business. He utilized me in ways that were more suitable to my skill set. He paid me to learn Photoshop and Adobe Illustrator so I could help him with the graphics and design aspects of his company. I helped him design ads and flyers for his business, which was my first real job, making five dollars an hour just to help him out, and it was fun. I enjoyed doing the creative work to make his business look good. I usually was interested in any creative work.

What's super interesting, though, is that the skills I thought I was learning just to help my dad turned out to be the skills that helped me in the long run: I now use Photoshop and Illustrator weekly for my videos, projects, and other entrepreneurial endeavors; and the real estate knowledge gave me and Jess a huge leg up when we decided to buy and later sell our first condo in LA, and then buy and rent out another condo in Boca Raton, and then build and renovate two other houses in Boca as well. Investing in real estate has become a passion for me and Jess!

Perspective is key when you're going through things you may not love at the time. Your future self might be glad you're doing whatever it is you're doing right now. So remember: You're not just going through what you're going through. You're *growing* through what you're going through.

Also, remember when I said earlier that boredom can be a great motivator?

Well, one day I decided to make my first Vine. I came up with the idea to play the music from *The Lion King*'s "Can You Feel the Love Tonight?" and show a quick few seconds from the scene where Simba licks Nala's face. Then I cut to me next to my sister in the bathroom, where she was about to start doing her makeup.

I told her I wanted to film something that would just take a few seconds (literally). I turned on the camera, then turned and licked her face with no warning and screamed, "Do you feel the love?"

"Ewww!" she said, horrified.

Okay, that definitely sounds stupid writing it out, and if I were to watch it again now, I'd probably still think it was stupid. But back then, I clearly thought it was a good idea.

I posted it, and a few people watched it and thought it was funny. Even though growth was slow at first, I was determined to make the most of this little opportunity Vine had given me.

That's how my career started. It was that simple (and stupid, lol). I came up with ideas and filmed them. You couldn't edit on Vine at that point and couldn't upload videos from outside of the app. So I would reshoot countless times until I was happy, then post the videos. My content slowly but steadily gained traction every time I posted. It took a while, but I didn't give up. I posted every single day and grew—a few more views, a few more likes, a few more followers at a time.

I started my first semester at FAU not knowing what I wanted to major in, just exploring the basic college-level courses. It didn't feel like a big step up from what I'd already been doing in high school—taking classes only once a week and then studying at home. So I dedicated a lot of time to making videos in my free time with a few friends who were also trying to grow on Vine.

At the beginning of that semester, after making Vines that summer, I had about one thousand followers. By the time my first semester was over, I had ten thousand followers. That was pretty great growth! But I kept looking at the big picture, knowing I wanted to be one of the top dogs on the platform. My six-month journey to ten thousand paled in comparison to people who already had millions.

Vine released in January 2013, but because of my whole not-having-an-iPhone debacle, I started late. Some Viners had grown to a million followers before I could even download the app. Regardless, I was determined. I wasn't going to let that get me down. And now, with perspective, looking back on it, I realize that being six months late to the game wasn't that big a deal. I started *so* early in this new wild west of social media, and getting to ten thousand followers meant I was off to a great start.

• • •

I wasn't passionate about any of the typical college classes I took that first semester at FAU. I didn't know what I wanted to do just yet. But I knew I loved theater, so I enrolled in a theater appreciation course my second semester, which was the only class I enjoyed. A part of me wanted to quit school 'cause I just wasn't into it.

My mom, though not entirely sure how to nurture my creative itch, noticed that I not only enjoyed my theater class but also "spent all my free time making these silly videos." So she encouraged me to pivot and pursue acting more seriously. I had loved acting since I was fifteen, and I was really into this mini acting hobby on Vine. Coming up with new ideas was creative and challenging, and I got friends and family involved. I just wasn't sure what my next step should be. I didn't know how to go about auditioning for movies or Broadway or anything like that. And quitting college definitely wasn't an option—my dad would never have allowed it. So my mom encouraged me to audition for acting programs at other schools. That way I could get into acting *and* get a degree (which would make all of us happy) while learning the groundwork of how to make a career out of this art form. That seemed like a good idea to me.

My parents couldn't afford out-of-state tuition, so I auditioned only for three in-state schools, two of which were exclusive programs that accepted hardly anyone out of the thousands and thousands of kids who auditioned every year.

I worried I didn't have the kind of training or amount of experience needed to qualify for those programs, but I gave it a shot.

I kept taking classes at FAU the next semester, getting some of my general credits out of the way, and while I did that, I went to these auditions. I did my best and I got in—to all three programs! As you know, I ended up at the acting school at FSU, which is one of the most prestigious and selective acting programs in the country. Out of the thousands who auditioned, they accepted only fourteen students that year. Such a confidence boost!

FSU accepted me into their fall program, which would basically be like starting as a freshman all over again, but that didn't bother me. I now had a bunch of credits that I could transfer over, which would put me ahead of my classmates, and I was excited. It felt so good to get accepted.

I was also excited about how things were going on Vine. By summer, I had grown my audience of ten thousand into one hundred thousand followers. (Believe me, I know that kind of growth is tougher today because there are so many competing platforms. Getting in early definitely gave me an advantage.)

My parents wanted me to work during the summer to help pay for school in the fall, but I told them, "I'm not going to get a job. I'm going to make money on Vine." And I did. In this wild west, still-uncharted world of what would become social-media influencer-ing, I had started getting sponsorship deals. My first was for forty-five dollars. A new fitness app paid me to promote it in a video. It wasn't a lot of money, but to get paid for what I already loved doing was pretty cool.

Early on, I set goals of how many followers I wanted to gain per day, and I became friends with a buddy from FAU who was making Vines too, so we started shooting together. I did anything I could to achieve the goals I set. People thought, "Wow, a six-second video. What does that take you? Ten minutes of work?" No! I worked four to five hours a day, all summer long, filming and editing and making every clip as funny and watchable as I could. My friends would call for a beach day, and they'd all get there by eleven o'clock in the morning, but I wouldn't show up until two o'clock because I needed to film, edit, post, and promote first.

It was worth it because my hard work paid off: before summer was over, I'd grown my audience to 750,000.

By October I was up to a million. Some sponsors were willing to pay me hundreds and sometimes thousands of dollars to work with them. It would take years for most brands to hop on board the idea of hiring social media influencers, but thankfully a handful of advertisers were hungry to tap into this new market.

I also offered something a lot of other Viners didn't: my material was clean. A lot of people on Vine used profanity. Some of the content was sexual or borderline racist. Not many advertisers want to be associated with that type of content, so being clean was a big plus for me.

Sometimes things pay off in ways you don't expect. I never could have predicted that my background and upbringing, including trying not to use profanity and trying not to bring harm to others, would give me an unexpected advantage in this world.

• • •

Out of the blue one day during this same summer-into-fall, a manager emailed me and offered to help my career. Social media management was a brand-new field, and he was a twentysomething entrepreneur just getting into it. We spoke over Skype, and I liked him. So I hired him! He offered to take over a lot of the business side of things and to try to get me better brand deals, so I was psyched. It was hard to keep up with everything while in acting classes as FSU, and I hoped he would make it easier for me. He would even end up arranging for me to make my first trip to LA that October 2014.

At this point Viners were all starting to tap into YouTube. The big difference with YouTube was it offered the possibility of paying content providers through automatic ads. So more views meant more income. It was the first time you could monetize content outside of sponsorship deals, and it was exciting to think about. So I jumped in early. I made a Q&A video that summer, answering questions from fans (just like every other Viner who established a presence on YouTube that summer), and it went over pretty well. Come October, a content media company flew me out to LA to an influencer event called Social Slam. I had dreamed of going to LA ever since I was a little kid. And now I was being *paid* to go there!

That weekend I met a guy named Kyle Santillo, who would eventually become my new manager and help me move to LA to live full-time. I'm a loyal guy, and I wasn't thinking about switching managers at that time. Kyle came out of the New York City fashion world. He just had a way of knowing how to operate, how to talk to people in LA, and he totally impressed me. But for all I knew he was just a good talker. A good salesman for his clients. There are a lot of those in show business, people who can talk the talk. But obviously I wanted someone who could back it up.

What you say is far less important than what you do.

I would want to see proof of his business savvy in action

before I'd ever think about leaving my current manager. But in life, it's important to take note of the people who cross your path. Sometimes they show up for a reason.

I went back to hang out at the Airbnb that Kyle had rented for himself and his clients that weekend. It was weird being surrounded by so many people in the industry. I felt like a fish out of water, but I left inspired and motivated. It got me thinking about what life in LA might be like if I ever had the opportunity to go there to pursue my dreams.

The seed was planted.

I came back from that weekend feeling like I'd downed ten cups of coffee in an hour. My heart was on fire, filled with excitement for the future. It seemed like doors were opening, and I kept making videos and working hard to make them good.

So my work was going well, and I loved acting at FSU too. I learned a lot in a very short period. It was intense and fun, and I was surrounded by incredibly talented people. I learned a lot from my peers *and* professors. It was also my first time living away from home, which helped me grow. FSU, where my mom also went to school, is in Tallahassee, which is about a seven-hour drive from my family in Pompano Beach. There was no running home to my mommy and daddy if I needed something. I had to figure things out myself.

Since nearly all my living expenses were built into the tuition and fees, I was able to save most of the money I made, which happened to be on Vine. A lot of other kids were working and saving money while going to school too. In-state tuition was cheap enough that I was able to help pay for a decent chunk of it, and my dad was able to kick in the rest so I wouldn't get saddled with loans. (My dad was strict about me not getting buried in debt at a young age like he and my mom did.)

I was grateful to have that time to ease into the realities of paying my own way.

While my work, school, and finances were going well, the rest of my life was a mess. This was when I went through that first relationship and my first breakup—the one I told you about in chapter 4.

It's amazing to look back on that year or two after high school. I learned so much, so fast, both in and out of school. And I think one of the biggest lessons that kept popping up was how important it is to pay attention to the positives that come out of my "failures."

Think about it: I failed my real estate exam but gained all sorts of knowledge and skills I would use for other purposes later. I also found Vine while in that class. I basically "failed" at going to college at FAU, but that led me to chase my *real* enthusiasm for acting and to my auditioning and getting into the incredible acting program at FSU. My first relationship was a total failure, but it taught me to look for red flags and make sure whoever I met next truly had the values I wanted in a partner.

The breakup also gave me the freedom not to feel tied down to a relationship when the opportunity came to move to LA and pursue my acting and social media careers full-time the following summer. If I'd had a girlfriend in Tallahassee, I think the motivation to stay in school and to stay close to her might have outweighed the opportunities that soon followed.

Why did so many positive things seem to happen because of the "failures" in my life? The answer is pretty simple: I believe "God works for the good of those who love him, who have been called according to his purpose" (Romans 8:28). That sounds positive, but the realities of it can be painful. That relationship and breakup were awful to experience, but God still used them for my good. None of the "mistakes" we make detract from God's plans. And knowing that makes getting through the tough times a little easier for me.

I don't mean I always have the right mindset the day something terrible happens, like the day I broke up with my girlfriend or both days I flunked the real estate exam. It takes a minute to get over things. Nobody wants to fail, right? I'm actually going through a season of quite a few failures right now as I work on this book (which I'll discuss later), and I often don't know what to do with it all. Both you and I need to know it's okay to feel sad when crap hits the fan. At some point, after the sting has worn off and the pain has dulled, I take some time to reflect on what can be learned or what has already been learned from a hard situation; I try to think about what the upside might be.

Focusing on the lessons learned is a huge part of what I think it takes to become successful.

Which gets me to the true definition of success, something I thought about a lot as I entered my twenties.

To me, success doesn't necessarily mean you make a lot of money, drive a nice car, or live in a big house. Success involves a lot more than that. The simplest definition of success is simply achieving the goals you set, right? You're a success if you do that. You're a success if you set goals for yourself and then go out and make them happen. But what goals are you setting? I don't think enough of us put the time and thought into setting the right goals. And if we don't set them, how can we ever be successful?

A lot of people make career goals: to get the job, to get the promotion, to make the quarterly sales goal, to win the medal or win the award—whatever it is. And those are important goals. But I'm talking about *life. If you don't have a life mission and purpose, I don't think you'll ever find fulfilment*, no matter how successful you are in business or sports or entertainment or anything else.

This might sound a bit backward, but stay with me. One of the things I'm trying to find success in is being okay with who I am, even when I don't meet the goals I've set or the expectations I've placed on myself. If I put all of my meaning and purpose in achieving my goals, where does that leave me when I don't achieve them? Setting goals and expectations for yourself is good unless you make them "god" over everything else. So even now, amid my failures, *true success is fully understanding God's view of me and that God is still so happy and pleased with who I am, even when I fail.*

Sometimes success is recognizing what steps you need to take next and simply taking them. Even as I've worked on this book, I've battled depression, and some days I feel like everything is falling apart. I often feel like I'm *failing* because of the depression, but Jess continues to tell me that she's proud of me because of the progress I'm making toward getting better, because I'm in therapy every week, because I'm taking time off work, because I'm eager to understand my issues, because I'm leaning into God for help. I'm still finding success, but in a way most people (including myself a lot of the time) would consider failure.

We live in this "go, go, go" world where people think nothing of telling you to work fifteen hours a day to achieve what you want, to get into the grind, to work yourself to the bone to achieve financial success. But at what cost? Money isn't the only goal, is it? What about love, marriage, happiness, giving back, helping others, sharing what you know, seeing the world, raising kids, finding faith, getting closer to God, being at peace with yourself? What about everything you want out of *life*? If the hustle is keeping you from those things, how is that success?

Any of us can choose to live a more goal-oriented life, and a more intentional life, at any time.

Look at it scientifically if you want. What's the rule? For every action there's an equal and opposite reaction. I think that applies to more than physics. The consequences of your actions come back to you. So what kind of consequences do you want? Positive? Or negative?

And this isn't karma, although I know people like to use that term. It's just logical. For example, if you start saving money at a young age, you can offer your family solid financial security in the future.

When I ask people what kind of a life they're choosing, I'm always surprised when they look at me like it's something they haven't thought about at all.

What kind of life do you want to live? Do you want to have a job you love, or do you want to have a job that keeps you stressed out all the time? Do you want a trusting relationship or to live in constant emotional agony?

If you're not choosing the kind of life you want, then how can you expect to get it?

Choosing the kind of life you want is a big part of the mission of life!

Part of setting goals is living *in alignment* with those goals. So you have to ask yourself, "Is what I'm doing leading me to accomplish the mission I'm on?"

You won't make a fortune on Wall Street if you don't dedicate yourself to learning the trade and getting into it for long hours every single day. Just like you wouldn't expect to become a world-class athlete without putting in time at the gym. And you cannot assume you'll have a world-class relationship if you're not willing to understand the other person's needs and strive to be the best partner to your spouse.

Sit down. Make a list. Not just of abstract dreams, but actual goals. Stuff you'd like to achieve. "I want a healthy marriage." "I want to live by the beach." "I want to not be resentful and bitter." "I want to have a better relationship with my kids." Whatever it is, write it down. Think about it. Then go work on those goals. Figure out what you have to do to make them happen. If you don't know how to do it, ask somebody—a teacher, a friend, a parent, a pastor, a therapist, a perfect stranger who seems to have what you want. We have access to all kinds of people on social media today. You can connect with people anywhere on earth. Try it. Reach out. You might actually hear back.

Reflect

- What do you know about your own family history?
- Have you explored your past by talking to your parents and grandparents (if they're still around) to learn more about where some of your innate strengths and challenges in life might come from?
- What does your multigenerational story look like up until this point in time?
- How can your family history inspire you to set a stronger vision and aim for something higher or better during the next chapters of this multigenerational story you're now living?

- What can you do to develop new skills that align with your unique talents and interests (or not)?
- Even if you hated typical education (spoken like a true homeschooler, right?), have you ever thought about learning something new simply because it's something you're interested in? Not something that's dictated by parents or a school administration, but dictated by *you*?
- What do you find entertaining? Is it something you could do yourself? Have you ever tried? Even if it's not something you want to do for a living, doing something as a hobby can bring joy and richness to your life, so why not try?

And I'll say it again because I think it's so important: If you're not choosing the kind of life you want, then how can you expect to get it? Ask yourself, "What are my goals?" Not just for work but for your *life*. I really want you to think about these and write them down. Then take a step toward making those goals happen. It's a cliché, but every journey starts with a single step.

SEVEN

Meeting Her

At the end of 2014, I turned my attention to making more YouTube videos. That seemed to be where all the big players on Vine were migrating, so I figured I should follow. At the same time, I noticed that the top dogs of social media were landing bigger opportunities, not only in the brand space on social media but also in traditional media within film, TV, music, and more. I wanted to compete at that level, but I needed help.

After getting some more sponsorship deals on my own and not landing any significant deals through my current manager, I decided to reach out to Kyle, the manager I had met in LA, to see what he might be able to do for me if I hired him instead. (There were no hard feelings. The manager I was with didn't stay in the business as a manager anyway. We were all trying to figure out this social media world. It was new to *everyone*.)

After several meetings and a bit of back and forth, I hired Kyle in February 2015 not only with the intention of growing my social media presence and getting involved with some better sponsorships and other money-making opportunities but also with the hope that he could get me some auditions and traditional acting gigs too. And he did! In May, right as my first year at FSU was ending, Kyle landed me a small part in an indie film *and* a job promoting a Disney film. *Disney.*

Oh my gosh! What a difference it made having somebody who was already a player in the business and who really worked for me and believed in me. I was so excited.

I was supposed to be home from college for two weeks before

flying to LA, but that was cut to only one week because of the Disney gig. Kyle and his business partners had just moved to LA themselves, and they were kind enough to let me crash in their spare bedroom. It all happened so fast.

The first thing I did when I landed in LA was the Disney deal. I went to a house and took some video and made social posts about the movie. It wasn't an acting gig, but it was still exciting because it was Disney. That was soon followed by a single day on set for a role I booked in a Blumhouse movie called *Like. Share. Follow.*, a thriller about a livestreamer. I played a fan of the main character, and they needed to get reaction shots of me sitting in a chair, watching what was happening online. Talk about an easy gig! It was sweet. I couldn't believe it. I was finally on a movie set, working under the lights, surrounded by professionals and real cameras (not my phone, lol). I wasn't too intimidated walking onto that set. I did have some nerves—it was my first speaking role in a legit film—but I was confident in what I was doing. I had been around a couple of film sets during high school.

I also auditioned for modeling gigs and landed a couple of background and extra roles in films that were shooting in Miami. In those films, I was just a face in the crowd. "Background" is exactly what the term implies. But this was the next step in what I wanted to do. And a year of acting classes at FSU definitely prepped me with more acting chops, which was helpful.

Then Kyle got me an invite to the Billboard Music Awards so I could post from the red carpet and during the show. It felt surreal. Kyle had some of his other clients there too, so I was able to hang back and blend in and pretend like I knew what I was doing. But I felt so out of place, thinking, "How am I here? I definitely don't deserve to be here."

A lot of us feel that sort of doubt sometimes, don't we? Impostor syndrome, they call it. The important thing is to push through it. If I hadn't pushed through it, if I'd backed out, if I'd decided to slow down and wait until I was "ready" or everything felt "just right," I may never have gotten the opportunities I did.

In June, Kyle landed me a deal with 7Up to go to Vegas and post about EDC (Electric Daisy Carnival), where I met Martin Garrix, one of the top DJs in the world. I ended up on the stage behind him while he was performing for, like, a hundred thousand people! It was so bizarre. That night I was without a doubt the most awkward guy in Vegas for the entire two minutes I was up there.

Again, I wondered, "How am I here? A month ago I was at FSU tripping over pebbles on my skateboard while trying to get to class."

I was amazed at how much had happened in such a short time.

A couple of weeks later I got paid to go on an RV road trip with a handful of other influencers to promote the film *Paper Towns*, starring Cara Delevingne and Nat Wolff. I didn't meet Cara or any of the stars, but I got to travel all over the Southwest and see the Grand Canyon for the first time—all while getting paid to do it.

When I got back to LA, I did some promotional work for Hollister and McDonald's. I was able to get consistent work, and before I knew it, it was late July. It was almost time to go back to school—but I didn't want to leave.

I was still living at Kyle's at that point, but I couldn't help but think, "I would be *stupid* to leave."

There was just too much happening for me to go back to school. I loved the education I was getting at FSU, but I looked around and thought, "The opportunity I have here now is probably as good or better than it will be in three years. If I stay in Tallahassee for another three years to finish the acting program, this whole social following thing could be toast."

For someone else, finishing school might have mattered a whole lot more. But for me? I knew I was about to get on-the-job and industry experience that I wouldn't have gotten at school. I was sure that staying in LA and continuing to work with Kyle would open all sorts of doors that I wanted to walk through.

I had reached a major fork in the road, and that is when it's most important to remember the goal and stay on mission.

I knew where I wanted to go, what I wanted to chase, so I chose the smartest path to get me there. My time in LA inspired me in all sorts of ways—acting-wise, production-wise, music-wise, business-wise. And I knew the vision. So that's the path I chose.

I called my mom and dad, and I wasn't sure how they would react. Especially my dad. He wanted me to be able to support myself (and hopefully my future family) financially. The traditional path for that was obviously college, so dropping out because of all this new social media stuff was a bit hard to understand. But they flew out to meet Kyle and his partners, Matt and Clayton, and we talked it over. I was shocked when my parents both supported my decision.

I was always open with my parents about my finances, and that transparency allowed Dad to understand the decision I had made.

After years of theater and acting training, teaching myself to edit, grinding out videos and building an audience, and after connecting with a manager who had what it took to help me succeed, I was starting to *make it*.

An overnight success—after all that time and effort.

• • •

Settling into LA was a challenge. I didn't really know anybody. I didn't have friends there, outside of Kyle and his team.

As someone who's always been surrounded by a community, I tried my best to meet people and feel at home. I wasn't dating. (This was around the time of the incidents with those two girls. You remember them, right?) I was open to meeting someone, but nothing clicked the way I hoped it would. That was good though. It allowed me to slowly grow my community outside of romance and avoid using a girl as a crutch to satiate my loneliness.

I made some professional friends, but the people in your work circle aren't always the ones you form tight bonds with. And Sebastian and some of the other friends I did make through social media lived in other parts of the country or other parts of the world.

I was able to find some community through Hillsong (a popular church with a big presence in LA). I knew someone connected to the church, so I met with them. I went to service each Sunday, joined a small group, and made connections I knew I needed to make.

I kept landing work, and in November, I was asked to attend the American Music Awards. The AMAs! It was insane to see every big music star you can think of. And near the end of the year, I landed a role in a live musical (of all things) called *The Passion*—a major network event featuring Seal, Tyler Perry, Michael W. Smith, and Trisha Yearwood—all about the death and resurrection of Jesus. Of all the roles I could have landed! God clearly had His hand over the whole thing: my first big show was to spread the story of Jesus on network television.

At the same time, I booked a major recurring role in a web series called *Mr. Student Body President*.

But wouldn't you know it? At the end of 2015, I needed to step away.

I had to get my wisdom teeth out.

I didn't have a dentist in LA, so I scheduled an appointment with my family dentist back home over Christmastime. I flew back to Florida and was laid up on my parents' couch for a week while recovering.

Bored out of my mind, with only so much Netflix I could watch, I decided to check my Instagram direct messages (DMs).

DMs weren't something I checked much, but with time to kill, I gave it a shot—and that's when I saw a message from a girl whose picture was just too pretty to ignore. A girl named Jess. A girl who lived in Australia.

● ● ●

JESS: On Snapchat, I was following a guy named Jacko, a funny content creator from Australia who was traveling the world and sleeping on people's couches. He'd been to London and spent time in Canada. My first memory of Gabriel was when Jacko stayed at Gabriel's place in LA.

GABRIEL: I met Jacko at the same social media convention where I met Sebastian. He asked if he could crash on my couch for a week when he came to LA, and your boy was flyin' solo now, so I didn't even need to ask my mom! He ended up staying for, like, three weeks.

JESS: Right. And one day Jacko posted something on his story, just being funny and stupid while Gabe was trying to work in the background. I didn't know who he was, but I thought he was so hot.

These are totally Jess's words by the way. In case you thought I changed any wording to make me look good. Trust me.

JESS: He was sooo sexy! But anyway, he kept saying, "Bro, we need to edit. You need to be working." My thought was, "Wow, that's cool. He's a hard worker. Who is this guy?" I eventually went to Gabriel's Instagram, where he would post Bible verses and stuff. So it was clear that he was a Christian. I didn't know anyone in LA, and I was about to leave on my first ever trip to America, so I messaged him on Instagram and asked what church he went to because I wanted to go to church while I was there. A few days later, he replied.

GABRIEL: I saw her profile pic and was like, "Dang, who's this girl?" And then I saw her DM and thought, "Oh, that's a cool question." I didn't answer her right away 'cause you never know. But her Instagram was connected to her YouTube channel, and her family was tagged all over her Instagram as well, so I could tell, "Oh, she's not a catfish." So I messaged back.

JESS: We went back and forth a little bit, and he ended up giving me his number and said, "Text me when you're in town. Maybe we can meet up." I was, like, wow. Every time I think about it, I am so grateful and sentimental because he could have just kept scrolling and not opened the message, and we wouldn't be where we are today.

To both of us, connecting the way we did was for sure a God thing. We never could have orchestrated it ourselves. But God was leading us to the next steps on a path we could not see. Sometimes bad or unexpected things—like having to leave LA to get my wisdom teeth out—puts you in a position for something great, or at least the next step toward something great. I mean, if I hadn't had my wisdom teeth out, I might not have been bored enough to go through all those DMs. It's just weird the way things come together, and sometimes it's beyond explanation. But I had also done the work, and stayed on mission, to be ready for this moment when it came. I thank God that I didn't get involved with any girl in LA, because if I had, my chance with Jess could've come and gone.

JESS: I texted him before I left for America, and he texted me back, asking to FaceTime.

GABRIEL: It was just another level to confirm she was for real and cool and wasn't going to be weird or anything.

JESS: Back then, in Australia, or maybe just in my circles, no one FaceTimed. I thought, "That's really weird. Why don't we just do a normal phone call?"

GABRIEL: I FaceTime everybody.

JESS: So we ended up hopping on FaceTime audio, actually. It wasn't even video. But we talked for two or three hours. He learned about my family, and I learned about his, and I remember telling my mom about the call. "Oh, I was just talking to an American guy."

Jess had been dreaming of coming to America her whole life, and this trip to LA at the age of nineteen was her dream come true. She had saved up for the trip on her own, which I thought was really cool. First she went to Utah for a week, where she stayed with a close friend she had met in Australia.

JESS: I'm from Brisbane, so it was my first time seeing snow. I went snowboarding, and I went to my first American college party. It was such a cool experience. Then I left to spend the rest of the month with my mom's cousin, who lived on the north side of the Valley (if you're familiar with LA at all). I'll never forget it because I texted Gabe, just like he'd asked, and he agreed to pick me up in the morning—it was Super Bowl Sunday 2016—and take me to Hillsong on my first day in LA. We kind of bonded on that because I went to Hillsong in Australia.

GABRIEL: We weren't calling it a date. But going to church just made sense. It was our topic of conversation.

JESS: Yeah. That's how I had started the conversation on Instagram.

GABRIEL: But I also thought it would be a great vibe check. We were going to church. So we could talk about faith.

JESS: I loved it. And then he took me to lunch at a café. During that lunch we got to know each other a little more. I was more reserved, so I think he was just trying to figure me out. I don't know. I just have great memories of that lunch. I remember thinking I never wanted it to end. But then he had to go out of town.

GABRIEL: I had to go to New Orleans for a week for the live broadcast of *The Passion*. Great timing, right?

JESS: It didn't matter. That night I told my mom, "I'm gonna marry that boy someday. Just watch." He was the dreamiest guy I had ever met. I had never met a guy like him before. From my first impression of him when he picked me up, he was such a gentleman, opening my door for me. I remember getting into the car and thinking, "No boy has ever done that for me." Obviously that's not a reason to want to marry, but it was one of many things. He was very kind and just so different. It sounds cheesy to say, "You know when you know," but I kind of knew. Well, okay, I didn't know for sure that I'd marry him, but it was just this feeling, like, if there was gonna be a guy I'd like to marry, it was definitely him.

I liked that he was up front and confident about his faith and where he stood with his values. Honestly, I had struggled in high school. I felt like I was the only Christian in my whole grade. That's nerve-racking sometimes, but Gabe felt the opposite. He was so proud and open about his faith. So that was one thing I thought was really awesome. Plus, I always joked that I was gonna marry an American guy.

I didn't want to leave Jess that day, but the trip to New Orleans (to shoot *The Passion*) actually worked in our favor. I had a lot of downtime during the day since we were only doing night shoots. So Jess and I ended up FaceTiming every single day before I'd leave for set.

We spent hours getting to know each other and just enjoying each other. She had a bit of a social media following too at that point, which was cool. She understood where I was coming from on a lot of things. For her, it all started because she posted a video of her dad playing trombone in their kitchen while her little brother banged the oven door shut over and over like a drum. It was hilarious and pretty quickly got some traction. It ended up going viral. (If you're curious, just google "oven kid video.")

> **JESS:** It was only a hobby for me. I had around thirty thousand subscribers on YouTube and ten thousand followers on Instagram. So it wasn't a "job." I was still in university studying graphic design.

If you go back and look at her first YouTube video, it's a DIY on making homemade Christmas cards. It's *so* cringe, it's great! (Not nearly as cringy as my first YouTube video. You can skip that one, thanks!)

I wanted to get back to LA so bad so I could see her in person again. And before my trip was over, I asked if I could take her out on a date.

> **JESS:** He got back to LA, and I think it was the very next day we went on our first date. He took me to the Malibu Pier, and we watched the sunset. It was really pretty. Then we went to Santa Monica and ate dinner. I had less than two weeks left in LA at that point, and after that one date we were both kind of like, "Okay, we like each other." And because we sort of had this clock ticking before I went back to Brisbane, I think that forced us to be intentional about what was happening.
>
> **GABRIEL:** We were both of the same mindset: A relationship ends in one of two ways. You either break up or you're together for the rest of your life. So—
>
> **JESS:** We had to stop and ask ourselves, "What are we doing?"

GABRIEL: Yeah. It wasn't like we knew we were gonna get married, but—

JESS: I did, actually.

GABRIEL: Well, we can't all be as cool as you, Jess! Anyway, we had conversations like, "If we're going to start a relationship, let's approach it with care, be mature about things, protect both of our hearts, and not just casually flounder forward and break it off after a month apart because it was 'too hard.'"

JESS: It wasn't all serious. We didn't spend all our time talking about our values or our future. We had so much fun just talking about everything. And Gabe took me to see some other parts of LA, and—

GABRIEL: But we had those conversations early, so we were on the same page about how we wanted to approach the relationship. We knew that neither of us was looking for a short-lived thing, and we both said we would only give our hearts to someone we truly wanted to be with for the long term.

JESS: It felt so good to know where he stood and to know he knew where I stood. That made it much easier to trust each other and to trust we had each other's best interests at heart. We had only three weeks together—one of which was spent apart—and that might seem like not much time, but it was exactly the right amount of time for us.

GABRIEL: Right?

JESS: But then, suddenly, it was almost time to fly home. I mentioned to Gabe that I hadn't been up close to the Hollywood sign yet. So on my last night in LA, he took me to a cool lookout where on one side you can see all the lights of the city, and then on the other side you turn around and the Hollywood sign is right there. It was really cool.

And that's where he told me he loved me.

GABRIEL: I knew I had these feelings for her, and I didn't want to wait and say it over the phone when she was back in Australia. I didn't know when I was gonna see her next. We thought it'd be at least five months. So I just said it.

JESS: I felt the same. I was totally on board. I said, "I love you too." That was a special night. My last night . . .

GABRIEL: But sad too. It was tough.

After just getting to know each other and sharing our first kiss, we didn't know when we would see each other again. The two of us would have no choice but to trust each other enough to navigate a long-distance relationship, from opposite sides of the world, for God knows how long.

Were we ready for that?

I prayed that we were.

JESS: I prayed too.

Reflect

- Has anything "negative" in your life led to something positive? If so, does that make the negative thing more positive than you originally thought?

- Even if you can't see the outcome as a positive, can you see how going through the negative situation might have helped you in some way, or maybe even put you on a different path in life? A path to something *better*?
- What if *every* negative experience carried a purpose? Would knowing that make life's twists and turns a little easier and less scary to manage?

EIGHT

Oceans Apart

Brisbane is more than seven thousand miles from Los Angeles. It's a fourteen-hour flight between the two cities.

I don't think it's a big secret that long-distance relationships are difficult. Some couples struggle to make it work when they live an hour or two from each other, or a short plane ride from each other. But ultimately, the measure of distance doesn't matter if it's not met with an even bigger measure of commitment, one in which both people also have the same goals. Making a long-distance relationship work takes a lot of effort, and part of that effort involves being completely honest with each other from the beginning.

Jess and I were open with each other about our faith. We were open with each other about waiting for marriage. We were open about our pasts too. I told her all about my first girlfriend and what happened before I moved to LA, which let her know that I was extremely vulnerable to feelings of insecurity when it came to cheating.

Jess's response to that? She voluntarily removed all the old photos from her social media that were taken with her previous boyfriend—not because I insisted on it out of jealousy but because Jess made our relationship her first priority. She wanted me to feel as secure as possible and to let me know that what we were entering into would not be a repeat of my earlier experience. She cared about my feelings and therefore intentionally did whatever she could to make me feel more secure. I'll let her share a little more about why she did what she did.

> **JESS:** First of all, I wasn't a social media influencer, so I wasn't into Gabe because of his followers. I wasn't into him because of what I could gain by being with him. Showing him that my intentions were real— that was important. So I didn't take a photo with him for probably three weeks. Even though we were hanging out and obviously liked each other, I never wanted him to think my intentions were anything like that.
>
> The second thing was, because he'd had his heart and his trust broken previously, I knew that trust was important to him. I knew it was important to do certain things that would gain his trust because he sort of had trust issues. I wanted him to know he could fully trust me, especially being so far away.
>
> So removing the photos with my ex was easy. But then one day when I was home in Brisbane, my ex texted to ask if he could borrow a charger for his camera. (We had the same kind of camera.) We were on good terms, and I didn't think it was a big deal, so I said, "Sure." He came by to pick it up, and we had a short conversation in the driveway of my parents' house, and that was it. But when I mentioned it to Gabe, it really bothered him because of the whole thing that happened with his previous girlfriend.

I mean, freaking driveways, am I right?

JESS: If I wasn't paying attention or didn't care, I could have just said, "Get over it," right? "It's no big deal. Nothing happened. It was just a charger. I was just being helpful."

But for Gabe, sitting in his apartment seven thousand miles away, it triggered those old feelings of something terrible he'd been through. I cared about him, so I cared about his feelings, and I realized I needed to show him that this wasn't going to be a repeat of something he'd experienced in the past. So I said, "Oh my gosh, you're so right." It was kind of a switch for me, like, "I see how that could seem hurtful to you, and I won't do it again."

When my ex brought the charger back, I didn't see him, and I haven't seen him since. That was that. That resolved it. Same with the photos. As soon as Gabe said something, I deleted them straightaway.

I can't even begin to tell you how much that set me at ease.

Being respectful of each other's feelings matters. Well, not just being respectful of the other's feelings but also actually *prioritizing* them.

Being intentional about giving your partner every reason to trust you, and then following through and showing that you're worthy of that trust, defuses any potential blowups.

Even if the feelings they express seem like no big deal to *you*, ignoring your partner's feelings is selfish. I mean, we don't even realize how selfish we can be sometimes. I think many other people might have reacted differently in that situation. Jess could have said, "It's just a charger. There's nothing happening. Get over it, dude." Which totally would have made sense from her perspective because she knew she could trust herself. But as we all probably know, proving that you're *right* isn't usually the *right* thing to do.

> **JESS:** It just was not worth him being uncomfortable about any of it, because I knew he was the person I wanted to spend my life with.

It's hard to put into words just how profound it was for me that she would prioritize my feelings.

I made intentional decisions to make Jess more comfortable too. I didn't go out anywhere with other girls, even as friends. Why would I want to inject any doubt or worry into this incredible thing we had with each other? I didn't go out a whole lot, period, in LA. I just wasn't interested in clubbing or night life or any of that. And the few times I did go out, to tag along with a friend or something, I usually found myself looking around, like, "What am I doing here?" That wasn't an environment that would help me achieve what I wanted relationally.

Jess knew I wasn't going around kissing girls or sleeping around or trying to date a bunch of girls, and that behavior was established long before I met her, so it provided a foundation of trust. She knew I was saving myself for marriage, and she knew that my goal for the future was to marry someone and have a *thriving* marriage and a family with a vision and love for God. But the most important part, to me, was to make sure my faithfulness and trust showed in the way I lived my life *right now.*

> **JESS:** I just want to say I think that's amazing. I never knew guys like that, who thought like that or acted this way, when I was growing up. And I love that he's

so open about it. I hope he encourages more people to
be like that—guys and girls.

Proving to each other that we would be faithful and gaining
each other's trust was easy because we were open and honest. We
were aware of each other's emotions as well as our own emotional
baggage, so we were able to deal with all of that without fighting
or stressing about it.

By getting all of that messy stuff out of the way, we were able
to establish a vision and some goals for ourselves instead of clean-
ing up messes all the time. We were now playing offense instead
of defense. We could charge forward.

As I mentioned earlier, success comes from accomplishing your
goals, and the goals you set should be intentional in every part of
your life.

We wanted a successful relationship. We wanted to make the
long-distance thing work, no matter how many miles were between
us. We also wanted to see each other in person again as soon as we
could. So we both worked to achieve those goals. The crazy thing
is, sometimes, when your goals are aligned with a partner's, you
accomplish them faster than either of you could on your own.

By pooling our resources and putting our heads together (along
with Kyle, who's been in our corner since day one), miraculously,
the two of us were able to work out a plan to get Jess back to LA
sooner rather than later.

We were able to make a sponsor deal with Hollister that got
Jess flown into town for the Coachella music festival just six weeks
after she left. And that's when we both started filming and sharing
the story of our romance online.

We had no idea how people would respond the news. We
were just happy and wanted to share it with our followers. But

something magical happened when we did: just by posting silly challenges and letting people into our lives, we got a lot of amazing feedback.

Jess had thirty thousand subscribers on her YouTube channel when she flew in for Coachella. By late spring, she had over one hundred thousand.

Obviously this growth wasn't something we could predict. It's nearly impossible to know what kind of content will work or what will resonate with an audience. But we were excited and fortunate to see this new audience respond to what we shared. We started doing long-distance videos together, and subscribers on both of our channels loved them. Our Instagram accounts grew rapidly too. Things were going so well that Jess dropped out of graphic design school, which meant she could travel to see me more and could do social media full-time.

We started our own Jess and Gabriel YouTube channel that summer, and it immediately got traction. Our content connected with people because we were genuinely ourselves and just showed us hanging out together.. We were humbled that people were interested.

It all happened so fast, and yet the relationship was something we'd both prepared for our whole lives. It felt like an answered prayer. Maybe it was.

My grandmother, my mom's mom (whom we call YaYa), used to pray for me, for years, saying, "God, please find somebody somewhere in the world for Gabriel!" She reminds us about that all the time. It's kind of an unusual prayer. I think a lot of grandmothers pray that their grandkids will find someone to marry. But the part about "somewhere in the world"? That seemed unexpected to me. And sort of specific. And now here I was, with Jess, who came from the other side of the world. Pretty wild!

For us, there was no better way to embrace our love than to commit to it, forever, before friends, family, and God.

So in September 2016, we got engaged.

JESS: We hadn't even known each other a year. I had just turned twenty. That's really young! So I was a little on the fence about when we should get married. We knew we wanted to marry each other, that was the main thing, and we hated the long-distance part. I had a conversation with my mom one day: "What's the best time to get married?" And she said, "Why wait? You guys know you're going to get married, so why wait?" That was such a blessing from her. Obviously, it would be hard for her to see me leave. But she said it anyway, and she made me comfortable with moving quickly.

My parents got behind our decision too. As soon as they met Jess, they saw what I saw.

Having our parents' blessings mattered.

And then—not that we needed it—we also received an incredible endorsement from our audience. Because of our careers and having a lot of our lives out there on YouTube, we posted our engagement video, and we were instantly flooded with support from around the world. So thank you for that, everyone. You mean so much to us.

We didn't even think about the where and when of an actual wedding at first. We were just sort of soaking in all the excitement for a minute—until we realized that planning a wedding across two continents might be a challenge.

We wanted both of our families to be there, of course, and our parents wanted all kinds of people that they loved (and who loved us) to be there, and we had to have our closest friends there—how could we not? But there was one big problem with that: America and Australia are on opposite sides of the planet. Sick. Which means our seasons are reversed: it's summer here when it's winter there, and vice versa. Not to mention the school schedules in Australia don't match up with our school calendars, and our vacation calendars don't match up at all. The only sort of vacation time that lines up between our countries, which was pretty much the only time we hoped everyone could get away long enough to travel to one country or the other for our wedding, was around Christmastime. That was it.

That meant that if we wanted to get married soon (which we did), we would either have to get married in three months, which is not a lot of time to plan a wedding, or wait and get married the following year, in a year and three months.

"So I guess we're getting married this Christmas?" Jess said.

"I guess so!"

We planned our wedding in three months, while still doing social media, fulfilling sponsorships, pursuing my acting career, and making time (and saving enough money) for the two of us to fly back and forth to Australia so I could get to know her parents and friends. All this plus trying to figure out what we needed to do for Jess to get her residency in the US so we could live in America full-time as husband and wife (which is what we both wanted) and yet travel freely back and forth to see her parents and grandparents and friends whenever we wanted. (We hired an attorney to walk us through all of that. It's way more complicated than you'd think. Or at least way more complicated than we imagined.)

It was a lot!

JESS: It's honestly so weird to think about. We started dating in February, got engaged in September, and then got married in December, all in one year. The craziest year of my life, and his too. We didn't even know each other the December before that.

God has a plan, and while the timing might have seemed rushed to some people, for us it felt as if we were following where God was leading us.

Turns out, it was a chance to fulfill God's calling in front of the world. To our shock and surprise, our wedding video—a nine-minute and forty-two-second montage created to memorialize our special day, just like so many couples make—was viewed by millions and millions of people. Far more people than any prior video we'd made. By far.

Jess and I aren't movie stars.

We aren't members of the royal family.

Neither one of us were on TV before it happened. (Well, I was on TV once or twice, but we weren't on the covers of magazines or anything.)

We weren't rock stars or pop stars who toured the world and played our music to stadiums full of people, or anything close.

So why would millions upon millions of people find the wedding video of our little love story on the internet and take time out of their busy lives to watch it, like it, and share it with other people?

The answer, I think, is a personal one.

For Jess and me, our wedding day marked the culmination of the craziest and happiest time in either of our lives (at least up until that moment). We'd gone from a chance meeting online, to private messaging, to talking on the phone, to meeting in person, to falling in love, to carrying on a long-distance relationship from opposite sides of the globe, to getting engaged and then married—all in under a year! In each other, as partners, Jess and I had found what we'd dreamed of and hoped for. And it all felt like some kind of fairy tale, like something you'd read in a book. (And now it *is* in a book!)

We feel so fortunate that this is the story we get to tell.

This was *real*. This was our *lives*. For Jess and me, our wedding wasn't a performance. It was our day to celebrate the miracle of finding each other. It was one special day to commit ourselves, in front of God and our families, to love each other and cherish each other and stay together forever. It was one more step in the journey of our mission. And maybe that glimpse of the miracle of love between two people in this world full of conflict is all it took to catch the attention of so many people.

Part of what God had given us was a platform to reach people, and I know from the comments and responses we got that looking at our wedding day and hearing our story gave a lot of people something they really needed: hope. That, to us, is a sign that we're living out our mission.

Sometimes I feel weird talking about our own story this way, but we all need to be aware of how our stories can impact people. God gives each of us a unique story: unique experiences, unique trials, and unique victories that can have a positive influence in the world around us.

There are few times either of us had ever felt as happy as we did when the pastor, my childhood friend Jacob, said, "You have exchanged your rings, you have exchanged your vows, you've agreed to marry in the presence of us all, but most importantly in the presence of God. And by the authority vested in me, I pronounce you, finally, husband and wife. Gabriel, you may now kiss your bride!"

We kissed as the music came up and our families cheered and the sun came out from behind the clouds . . .

The wedding? Yeah. That was the easy part.

The tough part wouldn't happen until after the wedding was over and the marriage was well underway.

Reflect

- Have you ever opened your heart to someone, maybe told them you loved them? Was it at all premature? Maybe it was one sided?
- If you've had a relationship where you weren't on the same page, what issues could you intentionally address up front in future relationships that would help you avoid the same scenario?
- Do you trust your partner? Have you been honest with them? Have they been honest with you?
- What could you do right now to help put your partner at ease (or a friend at ease, or a boss or business partner, or a family member, or anyone else with whom you'd like to improve your relationship)?
- What simple actions can you take to let the important people in your life know they're a priority to you?

NINE

Fighting Together

At the beginning of 2017, Jess moved out of her childhood bedroom in her parents' house, all the way across the Pacific Ocean, to move in with me. She moved to a city she barely knew, in a country she had visited only a few times.

I know I don't have to say it, because you're already thinking it, but the girl's got some balls!

The only issue was that once she got here and applied for her residency, she couldn't go back to Australia. Leaving LA to return to Australia before her residency was approved could have nullified her ability to complete her application.

We were told it would take seven to ten months to get her approval. That seemed like a long time to wait and a *really* long time for Jess not to be able to go see her family. But we were sure we could get through it. We were busy. We were excited about life. We focused on all the positives and did everything we could to make the time fly.

First, the two of us decided to make an album together. Jess had already been doing music on her YouTube channel, alongside beauty tips and lifestyle type stuff, and when the two of us sang together, we got such good feedback. People kept encouraging us.

No one needs a record deal to release music today. And we loved making music together. So the two of us practiced some tunes, rented time in a professional recording studio for three days (which is something I had never done before), and produced an EP of us singing some of our favorite love songs. We shot videos for those cover songs ourselves, we titled the EP *Under the Covers*, and we announced it to our fans. We uploaded it to iTunes and streaming services, and we released it on Valentine's Day.

Boom! We had a record.

Not only did our fans like it, but they also bought it. Our EP sold well enough and streamed so many times that it charted on Billboard. It's difficult to describe how exciting it was and how good it felt to get recognized for doing something we loved.

So that summer, we recorded a follow-up EP (*Under the Covers: Vol. 2*), which got even more attention and cracked the Billboard Top 200 album chart. Just as that album came out, Kyle and his team helped us put together a nationwide tour. The idea was to go sing these songs and share a part of our story with our fans in real life.

It seemed like a big leap of faith to me. I mean, people watching YouTube videos for free is a lot different from shelling out real dollars to come see us in person. So I was super nervous for a minute, wondering if anyone would actually buy tickets. But they *did*.

We sold out seventeen venues across the US. It was crazy! It all happened just as fast as everything else had happened for us both in the last couple of years.

We headed out on the first part of our tour in October, with three cities in California to start things off: San Francisco, San Diego, and West Hollywood. It was awesome. We came face-to-face with people who enjoyed what we were doing and had followed our story. Performing live brought me back to my theater days, and it was incredible to feel that kind of love and to share that experience together as husband and wife.

We had a few days off before heading to the East Coast, and we took all of that energy and focused it into finding a new condo for the two of us to purchase together in LA—our first ever real estate purchase, which felt so huge to both of us. Buying a place is such an "adult" thing to do, and the idea of having our own place was so exciting. Jess was into decorating and has a great eye for design, and I was into the idea of setting down roots and having a place that was *ours*, as opposed to her living in the apartment I had picked out before I met her. So we found a place and made an offer. Our offer was accepted just before we left for the East Coast leg of the tour, which took us from Freehold, New Jersey, to Cambridge, Massachusetts, to the Gramercy Theatre in New York City; then down to Nashville, Atlanta, Tampa; and finally to my hometown crowd in Fort Lauderdale.

The whole tour was super fun but a little bit nuts. We'd leave a venue at around ten o'clock at night, drive for hours, check into a hotel sometime in the middle of the night, then get to the next venue to start setting up by midday (or earlier if we had a matinee). Then sound check, then meet and greets with fans, then the show, then signing autographs or taking selfies as we got back on the van to do it all over again.

We didn't have a tour bus or a stage crew that went ahead of us or anything like that. Our transportation from place to place was a Sprinter van. Our tour manager, Kurt, was also our driver. Jess and I had one assistant, who helped with everything, and Jess had a hair and makeup artist with her. Kyle or one of the other team members from Scale Management was on the road with us. And my buddy Sebastian came too. He served as our videographer and also helped set up the stage and then grabbed a megaphone and went and hyped up the crowd before every show. He was awesome.

Traveling from show to show, we encountered all sorts of hurdles and obstacles, including construction on the roads, mix-ups at the venues, problems coordinating our merch table, and all the little things that go wrong when anyone travels. But I think Jess and I handled all of it well. We weren't like one of those couples on *The Amazing Race* that fights with each other under all the pressure. We supported each other whenever something stressed one of us out. It was all really fun, actually. Until we did the string of back-to-back gigs that took us from Nashville to Atlanta and on to Tampa for a matinee show.

When we were leaving Atlanta, some sort of confusion over the merchandise sales kept us from getting on the road until late. We got maybe two hours of sleep total in the van, and by the time we got to our hotel, we had only an hour to sleep before we had to get up to go set up the stage and get ready to play. And I kinda lost it.

I got to the venue with no energy at all. And I panicked. Thinking about going out and entertaining people was just too much. I told Jess, "I can't go on stage today. We need to push the show." I felt like I was having a nervous breakdown.

She went out and told our little crew, and everybody came in and tried to help, which didn't really help. It felt like even more pressure. I was overwhelmed, and I couldn't understand what was happening to me. I'd never felt this way before. I wanted to leave. I wanted to go to sleep. I didn't want to be around anyone, let alone get up and perform for an audience.

It wasn't just that I was overtired. Something wasn't right with me. It's like the whirlwind of everything—not just on the tour but in the past two *years*—suddenly caught up with me.

A half hour before showtime, it only got worse.

The hall was already full of people.

Our tour manager, Kurt, who admitted to us earlier on the tour that he hadn't had much of a relationship with God since he was a kid, finally pulled me and Jess and Kyle and Sebastian into a circle and led us in prayer.

"God," he said, "it's been a while . . . ," and just like that, he launched into the most sincere, humble prayer, asking God to forgive him for not talking to Him for so long and to give me the strength to get through this and for Jess and I to stay healthy and strong so we could keep inspiring all these people who had come out to see us. And his prayer worked! It was just what I needed. I calmed down. I set my worry aside. I found the strength and energy to get through the show. And it kept me going so I could make it to the last show of that part of the tour, where my family and friends were all gathered and where Jess's mom had flown in all the way from Brisbane just to surprise her. It was all so emotional and overwhelming.

Jess had gone months without seeing her parents. It was the longest they had ever been apart. So you can imagine how much emotion there was when they first saw each other that night.

The thing we hadn't talked about a whole lot was that Jess's residency approval hadn't come through yet. We checked on it once in a while. We reached out to the attorney who did the paperwork for us. But we still had no word when she would be free to fly to Australia again. It was frustrating. We also were given no expectation on what the whole process should look like and what would happen step by step, so we assumed everything was happening the way it should.

So as awesome as it was that Jess's mom came to visit, seeing her was almost like a big tease. It felt so good, but it also made Jess more homesick than ever.

I got through the show that night, but it wasn't my best performance, and I was glad we were taking a break.

It's weird. It's not like I felt like we were on the wrong path. I loved what we were doing, and I felt like we were following what God had called us to do. Even the closing on our condo felt like a positive sign: it fell on the day after that Fort Lauderdale show. Our bank had a branch in Fort Lauderdale, and we were able to go there in person to wire the funds in time for closing. That we were able to replenish our bank account with money we made from the tour made the sting of the down payment hurt less too. That put us at ease about the whole decision. God lined things up perfectly.

Once we were back in LA, Jess and I picked up the keys to the condo and rushed to get moved in by the time the second half of the tour started.

That November, we crisscrossed from Seattle, Washington, to Portland, Maine; down to Phoenix and into Texas; then all the way up to Chicago.

We finally came skidding home and settled into our new place just before Thanksgiving, which, although they don't celebrate it in Australia, served as yet another reminder that Jess wasn't allowed to be with her family.

This is when we became frustrated and asked questions about the residency process; things didn't seem like they were lining up correctly. Finally, in the summer of 2018, I went to another lawyer who was well reviewed and solely worked on immigration. At that point, after we had waited a year and a half, she knew something was wrong with our case and was willing to help us. Once we started working with her and she got access to our case documents, she saw the issues and told us what needed to be done to fix them—and told us it would take quite some time for things to be sorted out.

JESS: I was very homesick. So straightaway that bad news was a problem for me.

Jess got really sad about it, and I felt bad for her. I mean, who wouldn't be sad about getting that kind of news?

We were still so busy, though. We had so much to vlog about as we settled into our new place. We spent a bunch of time decorating the condo and shopping for cool stuff all over LA, and after just a couple of weeks, the place looked amazing. Jess is so talented when it comes to this stuff. It was amazing seeing her do her thing. But the whole time, she seemed kind of annoyed with LA. I thought she was just used to Australia, where people seemed much friendlier in general than they are in LA.

I was frustrated with some parts of LA life too. I mean, some of the clichés about the city are true: some people in LA can be super fake. Finding community was difficult and sometimes felt like pulling teeth. Plus, I missed my friends and family in Florida. So I figured Jess and I were kind of going through the same thing.

I just didn't get it. I didn't get it at all.

It was right after our first anniversary when we sat on our sofa and Jess started bawling: "I hate it here. I want to go home. I want to *leave*!"

This was it. Our first big fight. The one I told you about way back at the beginning of this book. The biggest, and really the first, fight we'd ever had.

We said a whole bunch of stuff to each other that we didn't really mean, with our voices getting louder and louder until I didn't even want to sit next to her anymore. "Then why did you move here in the first place?" I said before grabbing my keys and storming off. I left her there and drove around LA in my anger.

I didn't pray for guidance or help. When I'm upset or hurt or angry, talking to God is the last thing I feel like doing. I tend to ignore God and try to fix everything myself, in my head. And that doesn't usually work out very well, you know?

I couldn't seem to stop all these thoughts from spiraling: *If she hates everything so much, why did she come here? Why is she being like this? Why did we spend all this money on a home if she doesn't want to live here? We just put everything we have into this new place! Why? Forget this, and screw that lawyer. If it weren't for him, we wouldn't be in this position in the first place. I don't deserve this. It's not my fault she can't fly home. It's not my fault she can't see her family. It's not my fault she wanted to marry me . . .*

I was clearly frustrated and let it get the best of me. We're past it now, and eventually we forgave each other, but geez did I fail to love and support my wife in all she was going through. I hate even talking about this. That's not how I want to act or how I want to think or who I want to be. I'm so sorry, Jess.

JESS: It's okay. We both learned from it. We're better now.

Right. Sure. But it took us a while. And I hate that it took so long.

My anger dissipated, and I started thinking a little clearer after who knows how long of just driving around with no destination. So I know God provided some silent comfort on my drive to nowhere. But I came home and could hear Jess sobbing in the living room. It was awful.

I walked in and gave her a long hug. We both said "sorry" before we went to bed that night. We didn't want to be mad at each other, and we didn't want to continue hurting each other. We loved each other, and we said so. That was good. But we didn't resolve anything. This type of issue couldn't be resolved in one sitting. This became a pain point for a while, and we had to continue working through this over the years, even after Jess got her residency.

We were kind to each other once the anger dissipated, and we kissed goodnight, but that's, like, the bare minimum a couple should do. I think anyone who's ever had a fight with a spouse or partner knows that feeling. It's like everything still lingers in the back of your mind—or the front of your mind—and it doesn't feel loving. It feels disconnected. You might even feel like you're walking on eggshells. And that's not a good feeling at all.

A couple of days after this, I went to the gym with my buddy Chad. We were about ten minutes into our workout when he asked, "So how are you and Jess doing?"

I almost cried. "Things are so tough right now, with this residency stuff," I said.

He looked at how upset I was, and he stopped right there. "All right, let's go," he said.

"Where?"

"The car. Let's see if Pastor Josh is available."

Pastor Josh was the pastor at a new, smaller church Jess and I started going to together soon after we got married. Chad listened in the car while I told him what was going on and how I didn't know how to handle it. Then Pastor Josh made himself available, and the three of us sat outside a coffee shop and talked about it. What I realized (once I got out of my own head and thought about it from Jess's point of view) was that Jess wasn't mad at *me*. She had expressed her anger and her frustration *to* me. She wanted my support. That was all. I had taken her frustration and twisted it all up as if it were directed at me, as if it were all my fault and I was supposed to do something to fix it. I made myself upset and angry because I didn't *know* how to fix it. And that hurt my ego. It felt as if I were just a big letdown to Jess, as if living with me and moving for me were the cause of her misery.

I made the conversation about *me* when it wasn't about me at all.

Jess wasn't saying she never should have married me. She *wanted* to marry me. She wanted to live with me. She wanted to live in America. She just wanted the freedom to go back home too. A freedom that most of us take for granted.

Talking to those guys made such a difference. Chad knew what to say to me not only as a friend but also as someone who shares the same values I do, and he immediately knew who else could bring some comfort and wisdom to the situation. They didn't tell me what to do, or tell me what was wrong with me, or try to make me feel bad about anything I'd done. They just listened and gave me some support so I didn't get swallowed up by all the bad feelings that had flooded my head.

Because of what Chad did, I no longer had to try to figure this all out by myself. I wasn't alone with my own thoughts. When things get that heated, your thoughts can be dangerous. It's easy to wind up in a toxic place mentally, where your thoughts only add fuel to the fire.

Talking to a friend, and in this case a pastor, is kind of like talking to a therapist who's just there to listen and help, a shoulder to lean on. Guys don't seem to do that as easily as women do, but I needed that support in my life. It's important for guys to have other men in their lives who are understanding and who they can be honest and vulnerable with.

Chad and Pastor Josh helped me see things differently. And that allowed me to go back and start this whole conversation with Jess over again—not thinking of it in terms of "Why is she dumping this on me?" or, "Why can't I fix this?" but instead as, "Why is my wife upset? And how can I support her in whatever way she needs?"

I went home to Jess and asked if we could talk.

She said yes.

I told her I had spoken with Chad and Pastor Josh and that I realized I might have misunderstood her and hurt her feelings. I said I wanted to understand what she was trying to tell me on the couch the other day. "'Cause when you said you hated LA, I kind of took it like you were saying you hated living here and wished you'd never moved here with me and—"

"No! Oh my gosh, Gabe, no," Jess said, and she gave me a big, long hug, and she apologized for bursting into tears like she did. She told me she didn't mean to hit me with all of that in such a big tidal wave, but she had been holding it in for a long time.

"It's just that I can't see my family—"

"I know. And I feel so bad about it. And I don't know what to do to fix it—"

"I don't blame you. Not at all. I know you feel bad. And I'm not asking you to fix it. It's just, you know how my grandparents have both been really sick? I just keep thinking, 'If something happens to them and I can't fly home . . .'"

She started crying again, and we just held each other for a bit. This was so hard. Neither one of us understood why it had to be so difficult, and we were both worried.

Her fears and worries and frustrations were all valid. They were real.

What she wanted and needed was more support from me, more comfort, more understanding, more *anything* to help her not feel so awful about it all, or at least not so alone. Instead, I got defensive and angry and frustrated at her for saying all these negative things.

Today, I do my best to handle our conflicts differently. (And so does she. I'll let her explain more about that a little later.) This was the woman I loved. Why hadn't I thought about how tough it was for her not to be able to see her family? Her frustration had been going on for a long time. She'd dropped hints and comments about the things she hated about life in LA, and I just laughed them off: "She's just getting used to it, like I was when I moved here!"

She had said she missed her family, and I said, "I miss mine too." But my family was in Florida, easily accessible with a plane ride. I could *drive* to see them if I really wanted to. I could take a bus if I needed to. There was nothing standing in my way. But she couldn't do the same with her own family. She didn't have that option. She didn't have *any* option. If she went to Australia, she most likely would have been blocked from returning to America, which meant she would have missed her interview to get her green card. That's just how our immigration system works. It can be unfair. It's difficult. It sometimes puts walls between families, even when they apply and do everything right. And as we learned the hard way, one attorney's simple error can turn into a really long ordeal.

I had never stopped to think how I would feel if it were *me* who couldn't see my family. I hadn't even attempted to put myself in her shoes or to see things from her perspective before that fight happened. And it cost us. It hurt.

We ended up having a deep conversation about how much we loved and needed our families and how much we both missed our friends back home. Jess's family could only visit during holiday vacation times, and even then, it was expensive to travel all that way. They couldn't do it all the time. That was hard for her. And her friends had school and could hardly afford to make the trip even if they had time off.

Jess isn't someone who feels like she needs a huge group of friends, but the friends she had were *good* friends. And she hadn't found that type of connection with anyone in LA, in part because we'd been busy with work and spent a lot of time on the road.

We talked about going to Florida so she could get to know my family and friends better than she already did. And we talked about maybe trying to get more involved with church so we'd have the potential to form some deeper bonds in LA. But mostly we talked about how much we needed each other.

> **JESS:** It's funny, because in the back of my mind, I thought, "He already knows how I'm feeling." But he thought, "The more we're here, the more she'll get used to it." He was more focused on the adjustment I was making to LA and not the real issue I was having. He just didn't get it. Until he did. But I came about it the wrong way at first. I shouldn't have let my frustrations build up. Keeping your feelings in only leads you to burst at some point. And like I said before, that's not a good way to start a conversation. It's a good way to start a fight.

Ever since that day, whenever either one of us has something big on our mind or weighing on our heart, we speak up. To keep fights like this from happening, we now set aside time once a week to catch up emotionally with each other. We discuss anything, from something small, like what the other person did that bothered us that week, to bigger issues, like where should we live and how to manage the challenge of having family on two continents. This weekly habit has made us more prone to discuss deep feelings and issues with each other right away (even if it's not during the set weekly time) instead of letting things build inside.

Sometimes when we sit down for our emotional catch-up every week, there isn't much to say, things are good. But other times we need to work through stuff together.

Having an "emotional catch-up" may seem weird at first, but

it works well and it's pretty simple once you try it. A healthy relationship requires being open and honest, not keeping things in too long, and ultimately being on the same page with *everything*, even emotions and feelings, and operating as a team in every aspect of the relationship.

What the two of us would eventually realize is that this first fight, like a lot of fights, wasn't me versus Jess or Jess versus me. This fight was us versus the situation. If we were going to make this marriage work, we needed to figure out how to better approach this problem, and any other problems that come up, and solve it together as husband and wife—as a team, not as enemies.

It is important to make sure you're ready to listen to what your partner has to say and then actually listen without judgment or putting self-interest first. Sometimes your partner isn't even looking to you for a solution; they're just looking for your support. They just want to know you're both on the same team.

And being on the same team makes you stronger.

> **JESS:** I think, in general, even when we're upset with each other, we know that at the end of the day we're not leaving each other. There might be tension and we might be annoyed, but we love each other so much and are committed to this marriage. I know he's not gonna leave me, and he knows I'm not gonna leave him. I think that helps put any disagreements into perspective.

> **GABRIEL:** For us, getting married under God, divorce isn't an option. I think this mindset allows us to realize we are on each other's team, so we need to figure out a way to get through this together. Having

that mentality has allowed us to defuse things much quicker.

JESS: You need to remember that sometimes you're not fighting the other person. You're fighting the issue.

GABRIEL: Right. And there definitely will be issues. My buddy Chad told me once that if Satan sees something good happening in a marriage, he's gonna do whatever he can to stop it. A lot of these hurdles and things you have to work through as a couple will only make you stronger—as long as you're on the same team, fighting against what's thrown at you rather than fighting each other. You're working the muscle of relational resilience. If you work out correctly, you'll get stronger and not cause damage.

From the challenges of starting in a long-distance relationship to dealing with Jess's residency journey, I feel like we have been able to take those unique situations and tackle them together and therefore grow together in our relationship. Getting through those challenges as a couple has made us feel like we can do *anything* together.

Good thing too. We needed that reassurance and all of that growth because Jess's wait to get her residency would last for another whole year after that first big fight. And that was just *one* of the challenges we faced.

At the same time, something was happening in me, something that came on so slowly that I didn't even recognize what it was until it had already set in. I didn't realize it then, but the breakdown I had during our tour stop in Tampa wasn't a random, one-time thing.

It was a glimpse of what was to come.

Reflect

- Have you thought about how you fight and resolve conflict? With your spouse, with your parents, with your coworkers? What practical conflict resolution strategies could you learn so you don't hurt the other person, or yourself, when you disagree about something or when you have something heavy you need to verbalize?
- Do you have a community to help you when times are tough?
- Are you open about your emotions?
- Are you there for friends to support them through problems they face?
- How can you intentionally be a better friend? A better listener? A better partner?

TEN

Burnout

Toward the end of 2018, I hit a wall.

I didn't realize what it was. I didn't realize I needed help.

Jess was the one who finally recognized something was really wrong.

After another agonizing year of waiting and still not receiving Jess's residency approval, her family flew into town before Christmas. We all went to Mammoth Mountain for a little vacation together, which should have been a blast. But once we got there, I didn't want to come out of my room.

I didn't want to go out to eat. I didn't want to go out in the snow. I didn't feel like interacting with anybody. I wanted Jess to have a good time, to go ahead without me, to enjoy this time with her family. But me? I was just so tired. I wasn't sick in any other way, I just felt exhausted.

"Go ahead. I don't want to keep you from your family," I said. "I just want to stay in bed."

"You know what?" Jess said. "You're *not* okay. You've been like this more and more. It's been getting worse for months now. I think you need help."

I knew she was right. I wasn't okay.

"When we get back," she said, "you're going to see a therapist."

I had never been to a therapist. I never *needed* to go to a therapist. But I couldn't explain why I was feeling so down. So I agreed. We got a recommendation from a friend and made an appointment for January 2019.

Once I started talking to a therapist, I realized that depression had been sneaking up on me for the better part of the whole last year. Maybe longer.

I had been suffering. And I *felt* the suffering. I just didn't know how to identify it.

My therapist helped me to see not only how much the depression had quietly affected my life but also how addressing it and dealing with it would help me get my life back.

• • •

My depression started as a result of burnout. The crazy thing, the thing that surprised me, was I didn't *know* I was burned out. I always thought someone would know they were burned out. Like, how could you not know you're burned out? I didn't have a big realization, thinking, "Man, I need a vacation. I need to take a break from all of this!" I loved what I did. I loved being married, being creative, making music, filming vlogs, starting businesses. Every day was full, and it was everything I ever wanted.

In my mind, I didn't want to stop. But what I figured out (through therapy) was that not wanting to stop was more because of my fear of failure and the fear of not being who I thought I wanted to be. I couldn't "just stop." That wasn't who I was. I was determined to push through everything, no matter the pain.

My body and soul thought otherwise.

What I learned through therapy, after the fact, is that I had multiple signs of burnout, some of which also signaled depression. If I had known the signs, maybe I would have recognized them sooner and taken steps to prevent what happened. Which is why I'm sharing them here, for you.

The first thing I felt was disconnected. Even though Jess and I were doing great, I felt like my relationships with friends and even family were changing. It was almost like the more I dove into my career, the more distant I felt, as if my relationships didn't matter as much. I felt like friends didn't want to be around me anymore, when in fact it might have been me who was pulling away without even knowing it. I felt disconnected from everyone but Jess. I stopped wanting to get together with other people. It didn't feel worth all the effort I had been putting in. "Does it even matter to them? Why bother?"

On top of that, I felt unmotivated. I used to be the most motivated person I knew. I would get out of bed every morning excited to get to work and super motivated to build my career. But over the course of 2018, I lost that feeling. I wanted to stay in bed a little longer every day. I was less excited about posting new content. I saw everything I did online as a chore, like something I *had* to do instead of *wanted* to do.

I also didn't feel passionate about almost anything. Passion goes hand in hand with motivation for me. I was always passionate about my work and my music and my faith, and it all felt less engaging as the months passed. It's weird to say I felt disconnected and dispassionate about my faith, but after talking to the therapist, I realized that's how I felt. Mentally, I understood my faith and belief and why I believed. I still saw it as valid. But I had lost my fire for it.

Same thing with my friendships. Whether the physical distance from my closest friends contributed to it, I'm not sure, but my passion for being involved had faded. Again, I wondered, "Why bother?"

I knew I needed that support and interaction I'd always had with my friends. But I felt too foggy, too down, too disconnected to be passionate enough to stay engaged. So I dropped off. I stopped responding. I stopped calling.

Lastly, I got moody. I wouldn't say I was irritable (although Jess may disagree), and I didn't have big mood swings or anything. I just felt kind of sad. And one of the things I felt sad about was the way I felt: that I wasn't passionate about stuff, that I wasn't motivated anymore, that I didn't want to get out of bed in the morning. It's like all that stuff made me more sad, and then feeling sad made me less passionate, less interested, and less motivated. It was all a cycle, and I didn't even know it. I just knew I felt down.

There were other changes too. I wasn't eating right. I didn't feel like showering. I didn't shave. I didn't get haircuts as often.

None of those things seem like a big deal all by themselves, right? I sure didn't think so. And these changes all happened gradually—so gradually that they were hardly noticeable until they got worse and worse and I was almost incapacitated. At that point, I wasn't just burned out, I was depressed. And that's what my therapist tried to help me with. He encouraged me. Once I could see it, once I realized I had a problem and realized it was something I could try to address, he encouraged me to take little steps to try to recover.

First, I told my team that I needed some time off. I needed to cut back on my work so I could rest and heal. There was no way I could handle another tour. And while I could find the energy to keep posting a video with Jess each week, every other project needed to temporarily take a back seat to my mental health.

Then I started with a little self-care. I forced myself to get out of bed and take a shower in the morning. I shaved even when I didn't want to. I watched my posture and tried to stand and sit up straight. I know that may sound lame, but it made sense to me. It's almost like the phrase "Fake it till you make it." Forcing my body to act like it did when I was *not* depressed helped me to feel less depressed.

Moving my body helped too: getting outside, taking a walk. It seems simple, but it worked. And for me, going back to the gym and getting motivated about staying in shape helped to motivate everything else in my life. I worked out with my buddy Chad, which was an intentional way to reconnect with a friend.

Just as the burnout and depression came on bit by bit without me noticing, doing all of these little things turned the depression around a little bit at a time too. None of it was easy. It was hard to accept that I couldn't just "go, go, go" all the time, that my body needed to rest. It was frustrating that I needed to see a therapist to learn how to properly operate as *me*. I mean, I should be the one who knows my needs best, right?

Wrong. Jess was right: I needed therapy and I needed to stop and learn about my emotions. Therapy made a huge difference. I'm grateful that Jess saw what was happening and told me to get help. But listening when someone who loves you tells you to get help is just as important.

We need to listen.

We need to be aware that sometimes the people around us can see us more clearly than we see ourselves.

● ● ●

My first battle with depression took a long time. I started seeing the therapist at the beginning of 2019, and I was just *beginning* to feel like myself again by the end of 2019 and early 2020—just as COVID-19 hit and the world shut down, which threw all of our plans for the year into a tailspin.

I'm grateful I went through depression before all the craziness of 2020. All the isolation and shutdowns were just an invitation for my depression to pop back in and say "hey" again. But once I was aware of how I operate, what depression feels like, and what might cause it, I was better equipped to try to prevent it.

The early signs of burnout and depression hit me again toward the end of 2020, only this time I recognized them a lot sooner. I got help. I processed those feelings.

This time I was able to regain my motivation and passion a lot sooner than I did during my first round, and I went into 2021 feeling motivated enough to start working seriously again, so much so that I took on more and more as the year continued.

Then, toward the end of 2021 and into the beginning of 2022, I felt like I was getting burned out again. I could feel the depression coming back. As soon as I felt it, I reduced my number of vlogs and social posts. I looked at how many projects I was working on and decided to cut back. I was caught up in the "go, go, go" again, and what I needed was to try to infuse the things I was spending time on with more value, more purpose.

> **JESS:** The two words that come to mind when I think about what Gabriel's been going through are *purpose* and *identity*.

I didn't even know I was struggling with my identity. But I reached a point where I wondered, "If all of this were taken away, I weren't on YouTube anymore, whatever—who would I be?" I put so much of myself into my work, and saw myself through the lens of my work in a way that I could hardly tell one from the other anymore. And that's scary! If my work fell apart and this career weren't viable any longer, would I be okay? I know in my mind that my identity is solid with Christ no matter my circumstances, but in my heart? Yeah. I wasn't so sure. And that crippled me. I couldn't bring myself to go to work. I couldn't bring myself to read my emails. That sounds ridiculous, but I'm guessing maybe some of you have had days like that.

> **JESS:** Our job, where you have to show up on camera and put on a happy face most of the time, can be a real struggle if you're hurting.

I could go on and on about this topic, but I'll save the word-vomiting for my therapist. I just want you to know that struggling with identity and purpose happens. It's okay! It's natural, and if you're going through it, I encourage you to bring it out in the open and talk about it with someone who has your best interests at heart.

Doing that led me to understand a bit more about my past, about the way I grew up. Everyone has wounds from their parents, some bigger than others, and I had a few things to work through and mend with my dad. This doesn't invalidate all the amazing things I've mentioned about my parents throughout this book. Those things are all still true. But no one is perfect, and we needed to work some stuff out.

I did everything I could to try to take care of myself through all of this, including the steps I mentioned earlier. And I also did something new: I realized there were days when going on social media just wrecked me. So I cut back.

A lot of people struggle with social media these days, I think. We're all sort of addicted to scrolling through social media. Even when I know how I should be interacting with it and the ways it can be hard on my mental state, I still seem to be affected, and I'm often in denial until it gets bad.

I found I was spending hours and hours every day just consuming social media. I was scrolling and scrolling, not even noticing when it got dark outside. On top of that, I was consumed with checking stats and seeing how many likes or views or followers we got whenever we posted. Sometimes I'd be checking on that stuff in the middle of dinner, and then I'd lose my train of thought and disengage from whatever conversation I was having.

So the first step I took was to remove all the social apps from my home screen.

The apps were still there, in the library on my phone. But if I wanted to go to YouTube or Instagram, I'd have to intentionally type "YouTube" or "Instagram" into my search bar to find the app, then open it.

Maybe it seems kind of silly, but it helped. It's like setting your clock five minutes ahead so you're not late to catch the school bus in the morning. We all have to do things to change our habits, and sometimes setting the clock ahead is just the help we need. And that's awesome. If a solution works for you, do it. For me, not seeing my social apps meant I wasn't as tempted to click on them every time I picked up my phone. But they were still there, and after a while I found myself searching them and clicking them almost as much as I used to. So I took one more step.

As I'm writing this now, I don't even have social media on my phone. I removed all the apps! I need a break from it for a bit. It wasn't helping *at all* with my current recovery.

Even with all that effort, I still struggle. And I know it's been hard for Jess to see me go through this struggle with social media. She even cut back on posts to her own channel for a while, which made me feel like I was holding her back. But she's been great and so supportive.

> **JESS:** I want to be supportive. And it's not always easy
> to know what to do when you don't really understand
> what your partner is going through. But you don't have

to understand everything someone else is feeling in order to love them. Just loving them through whatever they're going through is enough sometimes.

See what I mean? For those who deal with depression, which sometimes feels so isolating, having someone who cares can make a huge difference. It helps you feel a little less alone.

Now, if we can continue to manage the line between our social media lives and our real lives (which is something a lot of YouTubers struggle with), we'll be fine.

> **JESS:** I don't think we struggle with it too much. But if we go on a cute date or if he brings me flowers, we have to think about whether our intentions are right or if we're doing those things because we're filming.
>
> **GABRIEL:** Yeah. People do want to see those parts of our relationship, so we do film them sometimes. We often have to ask ourselves, "Even though this is something personal, if we show it on social media, is it work?" And we intentionally reserve some things that are strictly for us to share together, so it doesn't all become about the work.

We could go on for hours and hours, and pages and pages, talking about the intricate, crazy side of social media and how we all struggle with it. But on the other side of the coin, it's such a blessing to have it in our lives and for Jess and me to have this for our jobs. Even in the middle of my depression and Jess's long wait for her residency to come through, we were able to build a house in Florida, move out of LA, and continue working through it all because we weren't tied down to a desk in a particular city.

Does social media present challenges that people have never had to deal with before? Yes. But social media isn't going anywhere. It's up to each of us to work to keep our lives and our relationships healthy outside of it, or alongside it

At the end of the day, you have to ask yourself, "What is my *reality*? What is my physical world, which is *not* what I see on the phone screen?"

We have the world at our fingertips now on these devices— all the world's knowledge, all the world's gossip, the ability to communicate without borders or boundaries, a constant influx of information and entertainment—and we want to make the most of it.

But we also have to create boundaries.

We have to look at our world and draw certain lines so we don't lose our souls.

I'm still in the early stages of figuring out how to do that even as I write this. But the steps I've taken so far are helping. They're helping me stay on mission to continue toward where I need to be.

Don't get me wrong, I love social media. I love making videos. I love doing all this stuff. But it's a balance of doing it and doing it well without compromising my marriage, my mental health, my faith, and my personal life.

I think that's worth thinking about in every type of career, isn't it?

If you're sitting on a pile of cash at the end of the day, but you don't have any of your friends and family around because you push everyone away, how successful are you, really? Even the number of hours that you work has to align with what you want out of life. I'm learning this one the hard way!

As I mentioned earlier in this book, people are often encouraged to work fifteen hours a day, get five hours of sleep a night, grind, hustle, just keep going until you achieve your dreams. And yeah, I get it. I was doing that. And I think there's a season and a time and place for working your butt off. But if that constant grind continues, it will likely come at the expense of other things that matter.

I know there was a season for Jess and me to get our career up and running. We went through that season and did well in it. But through my burnout and depression, we've continued to course-correct, and we both are reminded, over and over, how pouring too much of ourselves into our channels will affect us if we keep at it long-term.

You have to decide what you want to succeed at and set your goals accordingly. When I was young, I set a goal to read my Bible and spend time with God every morning. It didn't always happen, but setting that goal allowed me to spend more quality time with the Lord than if I hadn't set it at all. And now I'm working on my prayer life. 'Cause your boy can be one lazy bum when it comes to prayer!

To have a balanced life, and to keep all of this social media stuff in perspective, I can't lose those sorts of routines. I have to maintain the goals for my personal life in addition to my career goals. Both Jess and I see our relationship with God as a true relationship and not just a "religion." And you can't grow any relationship unless you spend time on it. If you don't talk to your wife for a whole week, that's probably not the best formula for a great relationship, right?

It's the same thing for all of the relationships and goals you have. You have to keep talking, keep praying, keep checking in, keep up the routines, keep the connection—all of it matters. And when you feel any one of your relationships or goals slipping away, there's a good chance you might need some help to do whatever it takes to get it back.

Reflect

- Do you give yourself mental health checks or emotional check-ins?
- Are you experiencing any symptoms of burnout or depression? If so, who can you talk to?
- Never forget that, in addition to family and friends, you can always speak to a therapist, doctor, pastor, or other professional to get the help you need. You might even be surprised to learn how many people you know have been through the same thing. And seeking help and guidance will not only make you stronger but also equip you to make a positive impact on the community and world around you.

ELEVEN

Intentionality

It took the better part of two years to truly get back to feeling like myself, to feeling motivated and passionate about everything again. COVID slowed me down, for sure. It probably slowed you down too. It slowed the whole world down.

But sometimes slowing down is exactly what we need.

It was during all that downtime that I learned I *needed* more rest, needed to refuel myself. I learned that I needed to *not* let go of my connections and my community. I learned that I needed to put life before my work (and God before everything) and be even more open and honest with Jess about my feelings than ever before.

Jess learned those lessons too.

Right before we completed work on the house, just weeks before we planned to move to Florida full-time, Jess freaked out a bit. She was concerned about the change in time zone and how that would affect her ability to FaceTime with her parents in Australia. She wasn't sure if Florida would be good for us. She questioned whether she had put her own feelings on the back burner to get me closer to my own family and was nervous in general about moving so far, so soon, one more time.

But this time she didn't let it all get bottled up inside her. The two of us went out to eat one night, and she said she had some things she wanted to talk about.

"I don't want to upset you. I just don't want to keep any of this bottled up, and I need to talk about it. Is that okay? I'm not looking for answers. I just need to get this off my chest," she said.

My answer? "Yeah. Please. What's up? I want to know."

I was more sensitive to her emotions at that point, and the approach she took helped me to manage my own emotions better.

We talked everything out over some good food, and neither one of us got upset about any of it. No raised voices. No tempers. No driving off in my car. It wasn't an easy subject to talk about. I hated that she still felt so conflicted about where we should live. But I was also more sure than ever that we'll be able to get through it and will adjust and find solutions that we can both be content with as our circumstances change in the next few years.

> **JESS:** I had a conversation with one of our friends about a week ago, and she said, "Oh, yeah, me and my husband argue over where we want to live all the time." And they're just talking about moving within southern Florida! So it's not uncommon for couples to have disagreements about this stuff. It's just a unique situation for our families to be across the world and that both of us are so close with our families that we want to be with them. It's probably the main struggle of our relationship, really, just trying to figure out what that might look like.

Just like my second and third waves of depression were shorter-lived because I recognized the burnout signs and could address them head-on, these emotionally tricky discussions that were such a big deal in the early stage of our marriage have become easier to navigate as well. That's the magic of talking things out and getting help, being intentional about the way we handle things instead of just letting life happen and dealing with the consequences afterward.

If you want something, you usually have to do something about it. Wishing and hoping doesn't necessarily move you in the direction you want. It takes action to get there.

There's a Bible passage I like that talks about the importance of action. It's James 2:14–17: "What good is it, my brothers and sisters, if someone claims to have faith but has no deeds? Can such faith save them? Suppose a brother or a sister is without clothes and daily food. If one of you says to them, 'Go in peace; keep warm and well fed,' but does nothing about their physical needs, what good is it? In the same way, faith by itself, if it is not accompanied by action, is dead."

I'm not discounting prayer. There are many things we don't have any control over, and it often feels like all we can do about most things in our lives, and in the world, is pray. Prayer is powerful. But if someone needs food and water, why not give them some food and water (assuming you have the means to do that)? *Maybe the answer to what you're praying for is the courage to take action.* If you're praying, "God, fix my marriage," maybe the answer is to finally go to couples counseling. If someone needs shelter, can you lend them some shelter for the night? If someone needs a car, and you have one to give, why not give it? Jess and I did this for a friend of ours. We knew we were moving from LA and eventually wouldn't need the second car. Our friend was in need. So we just did it, and can I tell you how good it felt to be able to do that? It wasn't like we gave away a Porsche or something. It was a nice, standard car that I bought when I first moved to LA. It got him and his wife through a tough spot when they needed some help. And they were so grateful. What a gift to be able to take action like that and to be the answer to the prayers of a friend in need. I usually don't talk about this stuff, which is why I'm only now sharing this publicly three or so years later. We didn't give to make ourselves look good. That was never the goal. The goal was generosity and supporting people we care about.

I think taking action matters in many parts of life. Just because you're married doesn't mean you don't have to put effort into the marriage and take some action to make sure your spouse feels like they're the most important person to you.

Jess and I made a pact early on that at least once a month each of us would plan a date night. I don't mean we'd get in the car and say, "What do you feel like doing?" "I dunno, what do you feel like doing?" before settling on Olive Garden and coming home and going to bed. (You've done that, right? We did that before we made this pact.) What I mean is that every two weeks, one of us would be in charge of date night. It would be that person's responsibility to come up with something cool to do, to put some time and thought and intention into planning a date. Maybe we'd drive to the beach and have a picnic. Maybe we could hike to a special spot to watch the sunset together. When COVID was at its peak, and a lot of businesses were closed and people were staying in more than ever, Jess pulled a mattress into the living room and picked a movie, and we did a little sleepover movie night in our own house. Another time, I fixed up the bathroom with candles everywhere so Jess could have a nice bath.

None of our dates are hard to plan, and none of them are very expensive, but putting in that little bit of extra effort to bring joy to the relationship can make such a difference. It shows your partner you're thinking of them, and thinking of the two of you, which always feels good.

I know I'm using examples from our own marriage, but we definitely don't have this nailed down perfectly. Life changes, things get crazy, we forget, and we sometimes let our priorities slip. But when we notice there's a problem, we've learned to take action, to adjust to better meet the goal.

Going above and beyond to bring joy to the other relationships in your life matters too.

Let me step back a minute, to the middle of 2019—before anyone had even heard of COVID-19 and life was still "normal." After waiting and waiting for two and a half years, we finally got word that Jess's residency had been approved. We literally screamed with excitement, and Jess cried tears of joy. It felt like we'd been penned up in a little cage and somebody had finally flung the doors wide open and let us run into a big open field under a sky full of sunshine where we spun around and sang "The Sound of Music" or something. It was such a relief, a moment of feeling like nothing could stop us now. We were free to live the life we wanted to live.

A lot of people might have immediately turned the camera on and shared this great news with their fans. But we didn't. We waited. Our fans are important, sure. But we needed to live with this news and take it in ourselves for a minute. And we needed to share it with our families first.

For Jess's family, we decided that the best way to share the news with them would be to surprise them. To just show up. In Brisbane!

So that's what we did. We booked the first reasonable flights we could find out of LA, and we kept our big news a secret until we finally reached Brisbane and filmed ourselves arriving at Jess's parents' house.

Her mom and dad flipped out. There were many tears of joy that night. In some ways it was even more emotional than our wedding. So we filmed and shared that moment with our followers, showing them the surprise and letting them share in the joy of it with all of the excitement that Jess's family got to enjoy firsthand.

Taking that extra time and effort to celebrate and surprise her family made the whole experience more memorable. And to us? Making memories special matters. Celebrating big milestones *matters*.

Why? Because you just never know.

We had no idea how important that trip to Australia was going to be. We could never have guessed that the world would shut down seven months later and that travel to and from Australia would once again be impossible for us, this time due to COVID. But when the world shut down, we were prepared to get through it because we'd worked on our relationships: with each other, with our families, with our friends, and with God. We were all connected, even if we couldn't see each other in person again for a long time.

Life is full of surprises. It's full of twists and turns we don't see coming. Sometimes great ones. Sometimes awful.

Being intentional about our goals and our overall mission in life is the best way—I take that back, it's really the *only* way—that I know how to prepare for those twists and turns. Having faith and friends and family builds resiliency because when you have these things, you're not alone. You're not alone with your thoughts, you're not alone in this world, you're not alone in a strange place. That feeling of aloneness goes away.

We're supposed to feel so superconnected by social media, but sometimes social media leaves us feeling all kinds of disconnected. We feel so far from things, excommunicated in a way, because we see so much of what's happening in the world but it's not personal to us and we don't feel part of it. So we *have* to be more intentional about keeping our real-life connections strong. Now more than ever.

I'm so glad I get to go through whatever comes next with Jess right beside me.

My pastor from LA, Pastor Josh, said this one time: "The foundation of the country is communities, and the foundation of communities is families, and the foundation of families is the marriage." Which means if marriages are falling apart, then communities are falling apart, which is why it sometimes feels like our country is falling apart. It just makes sense. Think about a high school friend group in which two of the people are dating. If they suddenly break up, the friend group splits. There's all this drama because that "community" has just fallen apart.

I think about the foundation of my community of friends now, since many of us are married and some are having kids. A community is being formed from these marriages and children. And if a divorce happens, what will that do to our community? So much could be fractured because of it, and none of us want that. That's why we support each other and talk openly to each other about the issues and problems we have and the possible solutions we can find if we go back to the playbook and trust the Word of God.

Nobody's perfect. We all have issues. We all make mistakes. But does that mean we can't try a little harder? Jess and I are dedicated to trying harder—to being open to improving, to learning, to growing—all the time. We're still young, and some people might even say we're still newlyweds, as if we're in the toddler stage of our marriage. And that's true, relatively speaking. But we're also dedicated to this marriage, not only for us and our community and our influence on those around us but also for God. True dedication makes a difference.

How many of the problems in our country stem from the fact that not enough of us are focused on keeping our marriages and relationships intact? How many problems are because many of us are not intentional about how we deal with our spouses or even our friends and neighbors? If it's every man for himself and none of us care about or respect the needs and feelings of our fellow human beings, let alone our spouses, then where does that lead us?

I get it. Morality is a tough topic to discuss. People don't want to be held to another person's standards. It feels submissive. That's why I like the Christian perspective, which provides a foundation for everything. In our community, if there's ever a tiff, a problem in a marriage, a problem between friends, whatever it is, we can all come together and say, "Okay, but let's refer to the playbook and see how we *should* be acting." Without that playbook, it would be tougher to figure out what to do. If I didn't have that sort of foundation to build on, then morality would be relative. Without the guardrails and guidelines on the road of life, I could say, "All right, I can divorce my wife. Whatever. It doesn't matter." But because of my faith, I'm reminded that it *does* matter, that it's *not* just about me.

If divorce sounds like a good idea or an option you can keep in your back pocket for when your marriage gets a little bumpy or you feel a little bored, you're probably forgetting the bigger picture. What about your kids? How will it affect them for the rest of their lives? They're going to be your grandkids' parents. What will that ripple effect do to them too? How will it affect your friend groups? How will it affect your work, your attitude, your ability to succeed in other parts of your life? Let alone how it will affect your community, your country, and the whole world. To be clear, I'm not saying to be miserable for the sake of others. That's obviously a no-good solution. But understand the commitment you make when you say, "Till death do us part."

Don't commit to a marriage if you're not ready to make it last.

• • •

Our career has always allowed us to work from home almost every day, which used to be uncommon. A lot more people are working from home now. Some days, when we're together but working all day, we'll get to the end of the day and feel like we haven't spent time with each other.

> **JESS:** We'll miss each other, although we were actually at home together—
>
> **GABRIEL:** The whole time—
>
> **JESS:** Working on different things. But even if we filmed a video or something together, we didn't have that—
>
> **GABRIEL:** Quality time.
>
> **JESS:** Yeah, quality time.
>
> **GABRIEL:** And that's so important. I feel like I'm getting better at it, making sure that we chat and just ask each other, "How are you feeling about stuff? How are we feeling about the house? Are you happy with the move? How do you really feel about being here?" We talk about whatever is going on in our life: "I know you were anxious today for a bit. Were you able to pinpoint what caused that? Did you do something specific to help you calm down?" Talking about what's on her heart and what's on my heart refuels the relationship, helping us to catch up and understand where we're both at emotionally, because *emotional honesty is where deep connection begins.*
>
> **JESS:** It's important to know each other's love languages. And "quality time" is my number one. He knows that's really important to me, so he's been intentional at

doing what he said: putting our phones away and just talking about our day.

GABRIEL: I don't necessarily need that as much to feel loved and connected. But she does. So I have a goal to spend quality time with her daily, whether it's in the morning over breakfast or in the evenings after work or whatever. I know that's good for our relationship and shows Jess that I love her. And that's another kind of goal setting: setting the small daily goal that leads to the bigger goal of having a healthy marriage, till death do us part.

Because our lives, both personal and professional, kept moving so fast, we were forced to do a lot of growing up and a lot of maturing real fast. And that's good because it allowed us to learn fast too. We've gained an education from experience that we've now been able to share with you and many of our followers.

What's remarkable to realize is that God has been there with us through it all. He knew we needed to go through these specific battles, even the battles my family fought before I was born, so we could learn from them and share them. And so now, even when things don't go as planned, I remind myself that I cannot see His plans, but they're *there*. Every step of the way.

I know that without them, this book wouldn't have come to pass.

Without His plans, which were there all along, we wouldn't have our story to share with you.

> The heart of man plans his way,
>   but the LORD establishes his steps.
>
> —Proverbs 16:9 ESV

Reflect

- What are your most important values?
- What are your boundaries?
- What views on morality do you share with your spouse or partner or friends? Are there differences between you and your partner's core beliefs and values? If so, how can you work through them?
- What little habits can you implement daily to help you achieve the bigger mission and vision you have for yourself, your relationship, and your family?
- How can you stay connected to people who will encourage, inspire, and motivate you to achieve that vision?

TWELVE

The Mission

As I'm finishing up the final edits of this book, Jess and I are expecting our first child.

I started this book nearly two years ago, at twenty-five years old. Now I'm twenty-seven, and my wife is pregnant for the first time. I could not be more excited to be a father, and I thank God every day for this beautiful gift of a daughter He's blessing us with. As I approach fatherhood, I've been thinking a lot more than I already had been about where God will take our family.

With so many changes in store for us, we've realized that Florida isn't the place we want to call home. We don't view moving here as a mistake, because it wasn't. Moving here was positive simply because we did it. Neither of us will have regrets or ever wonder what would have happened if we hadn't moved here. Moving here gave me the chance to experience what life is like in Florida as an adult versus what it was like as a kid. It also gave Jess a chance to experience time with my family in the town where I grew up. And the timing of our real-estate investments here couldn't have worked out any better, which allows us to move with confidence, knowing we can afford to take a risk. So we've decided to move to Nashville!

Living in drastically different places like LA and southern Florida, we've both learned a lot about what we want and need from our environment. Being around creatives in LA, surrounded by people who aim to impact the world through their artistry, was powerful; and being in Florida, surrounded by people with strong family values and community values, was wonderful too. But in Nashville, we think we'll experience both sides of that coin. We have friends there, so we already know we'll be surrounded by a community that will support us and our values as we start our family; but we'll also be surrounded by a city full of people who embrace music and other performing arts and all sorts of creativity as a way to impact the world around us. Plus, Jess has been drawn to Nashville for years. It's where she wanted to move when we left LA. All our previous moves have been more about me, but that is changing: as God has softened my heart to the needs and desires of my family, He's helped me fall in love with Nashville too.

This will be the first time in our marriage that instead of me bringing Jess into my preexisting community, we'll be growing our community together as a couple from the ground up.

A part of me hates that I'm just learning this now, five years into our marriage, but the fact that Jess had reshaped her life around my community, my environment, my career, and my country—where I was already comfortable—first in LA and then again in my hometown, meant she and I started our marriage from incredibly different positions. For her, it often felt like I was dragging her on my adventure rather than setting sail on one together. And that's not necessarily healthy.

In the book of 2 Corinthians, the Bible discusses the concept of being "equally yoked." For context, a yoke is a device used in farming that goes around the necks of two oxen, side by side, as they plow a field. If one moves ahead or falls behind its partner, they both run the risk of serious injury. To get the job done, they need to stay in alignment.

The Bible is right: we need alignment in our relationships as well. It's important for partners to be equally yoked in their morals, values, and overall mission and purpose in life. And for Jess and me, starting over in a city that's new for both of us is a way to align our hearts in a way we haven't yet experienced.

We're ready for this new chapter of new beginnings.

• • •

I've learned more about my mission and purpose during my time writing this book than I ever imagined possible. Especially now, with a child on the way, I've become more introspective about my life, my childhood, my journey thus far, reflecting on the good and bad, seeing what I want to take with me and what wounds to leave behind. If I want to lead a life that's meaningful (and I really do want that!), getting down to the depths of what it all means truly matters.

Recently, Jess and I took some time to go the extra mile, to go to a family retreat together one weekend in Naples, Florida, where we recrafted our family mission and put it on paper so we can refer to it and do our best to live by it every day as we move forward. Just to give you an idea of how you can shape your own mission, for your own life, and your own family, I'm going to share our family mission with you here. Just remember, the meaning behind this mission statement is ours. It's up to you to create your own, based on your own journey, your own family history, your own desires, and your own faith.

The Conte Family Mission

1. Pursue faithfulness and intimacy with Christ and each other
2. Always encourage every member of this family
3. Be a home and family to others
4. Always foster a peaceful environment

5. Live a purpose-filled, inspiring story
6. Be leaders through action
7. Be generous with our time, emotions, and finances
8. Be fun and adventurous
9. Make the world more beautiful through creating
10. Prepare an inheritance for future generations

After reading about my journey in life so far, I hope the meaning behind each of those lines is clear. You can see where they came from, why they matter to me and to Jess, and how understanding where we've been helped us determine where we want to go.

Reflecting on my past wounds during this process has been more painful than I thought, but I know my children will one day be glad I did. I want to honor my parents and my family in this book, and because of that, I think I painted what one could interpret as an unrealistic picture of a healthy childhood in earlier chapters. With that said, I don't want to ignore the truth that there are certain things Jess and I won't be carrying forward as we begin our parenting journey. But that's all part of the process. My parents gave me the awareness and ability to understand their journey and how it impacted the choices and changes they made when raising me. Now I get to take that a step further. I get to reflect on my journey and assess my experience as a child to see what I want to leave behind and change with my children.

I can't help but wonder what our life will look like as God continues to work in our family now, leading into a third generation, stemming from the intentional changes my parents made in their lives more than three decades ago. I'm so excited to see how Jess and I get to carry the baton forward to influence the world for Jesus through our family.

It's no secret that this recent season has been tough for me—dealing with the depression and burnout, coming to grips with my own sense of self, understanding some of the wounds I felt from the difficult parts of my relationship with my dad. It's reassuring knowing that, even after all this time, God is still working to heal those wounds, but I feel like I'm wrestling with God through a *few* things. Thankfully, I have an amazing playbook to go back to again and again. The Bible always reminds me that I'm not alone in whatever I'm feeling. In this case, I've realized that what I'm going through is similar to how Jacob wrestled with God in the book of Genesis:

Jacob was left alone, and a man wrestled with him till daybreak. When the man saw that he could not overpower him, he touched the socket of Jacob's hip so that his hip was wrenched as he wrestled with the man. Then the man said, "Let me go, for it is daybreak."

But Jacob replied, "I will not let you go unless you bless me."

The man asked him, "What is your name?"

"Jacob," he answered.

Then the man said, "Your name will no longer be Jacob, but Israel, because you have struggled with God and with humans and have overcome."

Jacob said, "Please tell me your name."

But he replied, "Why do you ask my name?" Then he blessed him there.

So Jacob called the place Peniel, saying, "It is because I saw God face to face, and yet my life was spared."

The sun rose above him as he passed Peniel, and he was limping because of his hip. (Genesis 32:24–31)

God touched Jacob's hip, and Jacob then had a limp for the rest of his life. Jacob walked away from that spiritual experience injured, but better for it. Blessed. Similarly, I'm walking out of this season injured, recognizing my wounds, but better for it. I've experienced God, and though it's been tough, I'm forever changed. I understand myself better and understand where I may have gone wrong and where my parents may have gone wrong. But recognizing all of this isn't permission to dwell on the past but to courageously march forward, using this understanding to impact the next generation. I'm doing my best to consider these new experiences, to understand them, and to let them positively impact the way I approach my choices in the future. I'm looking at my past, thinking about my own life story, so it can shape the direction of our mission as a family as Jess and I lead our new baby toward the future—toward more and more of God's goodness.

● ● ●

I know some people out there looked at the cover of my book and quickly judged: "This guy's, like, what—twenty-something? What does *he* know?"

I want to thank you for not being one of those people.

Age isn't the only measure of, well, *anything*. Experience, wisdom, growth, failure, new understanding, change—all of it can be had at any age. We've had experiences that other people, even older people, may have not experienced.

I'm not trying to look extra smart or anything, because most of the time I'm not necessarily the sharpest tool in the shed. But I don't want to overlook any experiences and learning opportunities

I've had during my time here on earth. We've all had a lot of experiences by the time we're in our mid- to late twenties, and we shouldn't be afraid or ashamed to look back on them both lovingly and critically, allowing ourselves to learn from our mistakes and then take our findings and share them with others. Our experience growing up in this time, with the technologies we have and the world being the way it is, is in many ways entirely different from the experience of people older than us. This makes our experience unique and potentially *important* for those older than us to learn from as well. So let's stop counting ourselves out and start encouraging others confidently.

We also shouldn't go around assuming we're "just getting started" at this age and have plenty of time left. (I'm speaking to the choir here, being twenty-seven and old as ever! lol) None of us know what God has in store for us. That's why as I turn the page into my next quarter century, and the start of my new journey as a father, I'm bringing more intentionality to every bit of my life that I can. And I'm excited about continuing to share my journey with you.

In general, we're blessed with longer lives today than our grandparents and great-grandparents were able to enjoy. Let's not waste that. Let's make the most of it, starting today.

I think the more we share our journeys with each other as we try to make the most of our lives, living our lives with purpose, the higher we'll all climb.

So if you've been inspired or empowered by anything you've read in this book, confidently take the baton and inspire others: on social media, in person, at school, wherever. If you've taken even one piece of advice about being more intentional in your personal relationships, or changing your relationship with social media, or even going so far as maybe picking up a Bible for the first time—even if it's the smallest thing, it's *huge* to me. So thank you—

JESS: From the bottom of our hearts.

Thank you, thank you, *thank you* for listening and watching and taking to heart anything we've been able to share with you.

Like I said early on, I don't feel any different from anyone else my age. I'm going through the ups and downs. I definitely feel the pressure, and I've felt the depression and anxiety too. The only real difference is some of the guidance I was given early on. And I've chosen to align with that guidance, which has given me more time and energy to spend on the things I *want* to embrace, rather than spending it dealing with the heartaches and messes some other choices might have brought my way.

> The way of a fool is right in his own eyes,
> but a wise man listens to advice.
>
> —Proverbs 12:15 ESV

I don't know about you, but I want to be that wise man.

Ask questions, be curious, seek guidance. That's it. Don't spend so much time staring at screens that you don't allow your mind to take a break. Embrace some boredom. Allow yourself some space and time to think—and to be inspired. Pay attention to what you're feeling. Be curious about how others feel too. And don't be afraid to talk about it.

As a good friend of mine in Nashville once told me, "Notice what you're noticing." Pay attention to your life, your actions, and your responses—to everything!

Being intentional about my decisions, my goals, and the type of success I want out of my one life has made all the difference.

So I hope you'll be intentional about the decisions you make for your life too.

Intentionality changes everything. It really does.

Which brings me right back to the question I asked you at the end of chapter 2:

What are you going to do next with this miracle you've been given?

Acknowledgments

Mark Dagostino, thank you for all the hours and hours helping me take all my personal stories and sometimes incoherent thoughts and compiling something beautiful, something I'm so proud of and so excited to share with my future children and grandchildren one day.

Thank you, Kyle and everyone on the Scale Management team, for believing in my story and message even before I believed in it myself and for pushing me to share it in this form with the world.

Thank you, Anthony Mattero and the whole team at CAA, for putting together all the pieces on the business side, connecting me with all the right people along the way to make this book see the light of day and overall just being such massive advocates for the message I wanted to share.

Thank you, Carolyn McCready and the entire Zondervan crew, for truly believing in my story and genuinely wanting to be a part of the team that worked so hard to get this into hands and homes around the world.

To all the people who have shaped me and made an everlasting impact on my heart and mind. My family: Mom and Dad, Claudio and Madi, Sofia, Nico, Yaya and Yayo, Russ and Janine, Toby and Sarah, Tony and all my other aunts, uncles, and cousins (who are too many to name, lol) . . . thank you. My community, friends, and mentors: all my Florida friends I grew up with (you know who you are!), Sebastian, Bobby, Jake, Warren, Zac, Chad and Tori, Pastor Josh, Denny, Jacko, Roy, Ashley, and the whole Integrated men's group . . . thank you.

Lastly, but most importantly, thank you, God. Thank you for pursuing my soul and giving me the desires of my heart, for giving me an emotional depth that allows me to better connect with you and the world you put me in, and for a creative ability that I get to use for your glory. Again, thank you, God.

From the Publisher

GREAT BOOKS
ARE EVEN BETTER WHEN THEY'RE SHARED!

Help other readers find this one:

- Post a review at your favorite online bookseller

- Post a picture on a social media account and share why you enjoyed it

- Send a note to a friend who would also love it—or better yet, give them a copy

Thanks for reading!